1 PETER

NCCS | New Covenant Commentary Series

The New Covenant Commentary Series (NCCS) is designed for ministers and students who require a commentary that interacts with the text and context of each New Testament book and pays specific attention to the impact of the text upon the faith and praxis of contemporary faith communities.

The NCCS has a number of distinguishing features. First, the contributors come from a diverse array of backgrounds in regards to their Christian denominations and countries of origin. Unlike many commentary series that tout themselves as international the NCCS can truly boast of a genuinely international cast of contributors with authors drawn from every continent of the world (except Antarctica) including countries such as the United States, Australia, the United Kingdom, Kenya, India, Singapore, and Korea. We intend the NCCS to engage in the task of biblical interpretation and theological reflection from the perspective of the global church. Second, the volumes in this series are not verse-by-verse commentaries, but they focus on larger units of text in order to explicate and interpret the story in the text as opposed to some often atomistic approaches. Third, a further aim of these volumes is to provide an occasion for authors to reflect on how the New Testament impacts the life, faith, ministry, and witness of the New Covenant Community today. This occurs periodically under the heading of "Fusing the Horizons and Forming the Community." Here authors provide windows into community formation (how the text shapes the mission and character of the believing community) and ministerial formation (how the text shapes the ministry of Christian leaders).

It is our hope that these volumes will represent serious engagements with the New Testament writings, done in the context of faith, in service of the church, and for the glorification of God.

Series Editors:
Michael F. Bird (Ridley College, Parkville, VIC, Australia)
Craig Keener (Asbury Theological Seminary, Wilmore, KY, USA)

Titles in this series:
Mark Kim Huat Tan
Luke Diane Chen
John Jey J. Kanagaraj
Acts Youngmo Cho and Hyung Dae Park
Romans Craig Keener
1 Corinthians B. J. Oropeza
Galatians Jarvis J. Williams
Ephesians Lynn Cohick
Philippians Linda L. Belleville
Colossians and Philemon Michael F. Bird
1–2 Thessalonians Nijay K. Gupta
1 Timothy Aída Besançon-Spencer
2 Timothy and Titus Aída Besançon-Spencer
James Ruth Anne Reese
The Epistle of John Samuel M. Ngewa
Jude and 2 Peter Andrew Mbuvi
Revelation Gordon Fee

Forthcoming titles:
Matthew Catherine Sider-Hamilton
2 Corinthians J. Ayodeji Adewuya
Hebrews Cynthia Long Westfall

1 PETER
A New Covenant Commentary

Sean du Toit

CASCADE *Books* • Eugene, Oregon

1 PETER
A New Covenant Commentary

New Covenant Commentary Series

Copyright © 2025 Sean du Toit. All rights reserved. Except for brief quotations in critical publications or reviews, no part of this book may be reproduced in any manner without prior written permission from the publisher. Write: Permissions, Wipf and Stock Publishers, 199 W. 8th Ave., Suite 3, Eugene, OR 97401.

Cascade Books
An Imprint of Wipf and Stock Publishers
199 W. 8th Ave., Suite 3
Eugene, OR 97401

www.wipfandstock.com

PAPERBACK ISBN: 978-1-6667-3964-0
HARDCOVER ISBN: 978-1-6667-3965-7
EBOOK ISBN: 978-1-6667-3966-4

Cataloguing-in-Publication data:

Names: du Toit, Sean [author].

Title: 1 Peter / by Sean du Toit.

Description: Eugene, OR: Cascade Books, 2025 | Series: New Covenant Commentary Series | Includes bibliographical references and index.

Identifiers: ISBN 978-1-6667-3964-0 (paperback) | ISBN 978-1-6667-3965-7 (hardcover) | ISBN 978-1-6667-3966-4 (ebook)

Subjects: LCSH: Bible.—Peter, 1st—Criticism, interpretation, etc. | Commentaries. | Bible.—Peter, 1st—Criticism, interpretation, etc.

Classification: BS2795.3 D88 2025 (paperback) | BS2795.3 (ebook)

VERSION NUMBER 06/24/25

CONTENTS

Preface ix
Abbreviations xi

Introductory Issues 1
  Authorship and Date 1
  Audience 4
  Situation 6
  The Approach of this Commentary 10
Letter Opening and Greeting (1:1–2) 13
Praise to God the Great Benefactor (1:3–12) 17
  A Living Hope (1:3–5) 17
  A Testing Present (1:6–9) 20
  A Past Fulfilled (1:10–12) 23
    Fusing the Horizon 27
Holy Living for a Holy God (1:13—2:10) 28
  Be Holy Because God is Holy (1:13–16) 28
    EXCURSUS: HOLINESS AND SEPARATION 31
    Fusing the Horizon 34
  The Impartial Judge (1:17–21) 35
    Fusing the Horizon 39
  New Life, New Family, Same Gospel (1:22–25) 39

Contents

New Covenant Asceticism (2:1–3)	41
New Covenant Community (2:4–10)	44
Fusing the Horizon	52
Negotiating Life Honorably Among the Pagans (2:11—3:12)	54
Negotiating Life with Honorable Conduct (2:11-12)	54
EXCURSUS: MISSION AND ETHICS	57
Negotiating Life with the World (2:13-17)	60
EXCURSUS: FULFILLING ONE'S DUTY AS A CHRISTIAN	61
Negotiating Life as a Household-Slave (2:18-20)	64
The Example of Jesus (2:21-25)	68
Fusing the Horizon	73
Holy Living in the Home (3:1-7)	74
Missional Wives in Pagan Homes (3:1-2)	74
Fusing the Horizon	76
Character and Conduct in the Household (3:3-4)	78
Holy Women in the Household (3:5-6)	79
Holy Men in the Household (3:7)	82
Characteristics of Holy Living (3:8-12)	84
Fusing the Horizon	88
Exhortations to Communal Flourishing Amidst Opposition (3:13—5:11)	90
A Holy Life Amidst Suffering (3:13-17)	90
EXCURSUS: BENEFICIAL DEEDS IN 1 PETER	93
The Example of Jesus (3:18-22)	95
Fusing the Horizon	100
Forsaking a Life of Vice (4:1-6)	101
Life in God's Household (4:7-11)	106
Fusing the Horizon	109
Remain Faithful Even Though It Incurs Suffering (4:12-19)	110
Fusing the Horizon	114

Leaders and Followers in the Household of God (5:1–5)	116
Fusing the Horizon	120
Final Exhortations to Trust God Despite Opposition (5:6–11)	122
Closing Exhortation and Greeting (5:12–14)	126
Fusing the Horizon	128
Bibliography	131
Subject Index	139
Author Index	145
Scripture Index	149

PREFACE

Writing this commentary has been an adventure. Firstly, I realized soon into the writing process that even though I had spent many years in this letter, there was so much more to learn, to grapple with, and to consider. A pandemic with lockdowns and new levels of universal anxiety, not to mention limited access to resources, made the process difficult at various turns. I did not realize how exhilarating and difficult it would be, often at the same time! Secondly, writing a commentary is a somewhat lonely experience. Sitting in my office, away from the communities of faith this letter was meant to nourish and nurture, seemed a bit ironic. And yet it was in that isolation I discovered the voices and guides of those mentioned in the bibliography. I am so grateful for the work of scholars, past and present, on this epistle. Thirdly, I hope that this commentary will help those who follow Jesus. It has been enormously helpful in my own discipleship and with the communities of faith that I have the privilege of serving. I pray that God uses this to stir his people to greater faithfulness.

In 2008, I read a manuscript for a commentary on Colossians and Philemon for a new series called New Covenant Commentary Series by Michael F. Bird. I was pastoring a church and preaching through Colossians at that time. I found it a beneficial commentary that unpacked the text and pointed me in directions about its continuing significance and implications. I wondered if one day I might write such a commentary. This is the realization of that dream, and with it I offer my sincere gratitude to the series editors, Michael Bird and Craig Keener, for their invitation to write on the superb epistle of 1 Peter.

My interdenominational journey has been a beneficial one, and I have been fortunate to have good scholars inform and challenge my thinking. Particularly helpful to me have been Mark Keown, George Wieland, and Paul Trebilco. While they should not be held responsible for my shortcomings,

I know this manuscript is better because of their encouragement, example, and teaching. Along the way, I have also had the privilege of having some of my close friends read and respond to this commentary in either written or spoken formats. I am particularly grateful to Dawn Dalloway, Steve Batten, Gareth Naude, and Mark Pierson. My gratitude for them is enormous. My deepest thanks are owed to Sue, my wife, and my wonderful daughters, Ava and Mia. They provide so much joy and meaning to my life. I am grateful to have not sacrificed time with them to sit in my office and work. Sometimes we forget that it takes a community to form a Christian, and I have had the privilege of being part of some remarkable churches that have shaped and informed my faith. In that light, this commentary is dedicated to the communities of faith that have nurtured and sustained my family's fidelity to Jesus: Helderberg Christian Church (Somerset West); New Hope Fellowship (Onehunga); Primal (Somerset West), Common Ground (Auckland), St. Luke's (Tauranga), Rhythms of Grace (Auckland), and Connect Church (Timaru). May God continue to be relentlessly faithful as we pursue and parade his magnificent grace to us.

ABBREVIATIONS

ANTC	Abingdon New Testament Commentary
BBR	Bulletin of Biblical Research
BDAG	Walter Bauer, Frederick W. Danker, W. F. Arndt, and F. W. Gingrich. *Greek–English Lexicon of the New Testament and Other Early Christian Literature*. 3rd ed. Chicago: University of Chicago Press, 2000.
BECNT	Baker Exegetical Commentary on the New Testament
BSNTS	Bulletin of the Studiorum Novi Testamenti Societas
CBR	Currents of Biblical Research
CBQ	Catholic Biblical Quarterly
CEB	Contemporary English Bible
CTJ	Calvin Theological Journal
ExpTim	Expository Times
FN	Filología Neotestamentaria
HTR	Harvard Theological Review
ICC	International Critical Commentary
IVPNTC	InterVarsity Press New Testament Commentary
JBL	Journal of Biblical Literature
JGRChJ	Journal of Greco-Roman Christianity and Judaism
JSNT	Journal for the Study of the New Testament
JTS	Journal of Theological Studies
KJV	King James Version
LCL	Loeb Classical Library

LNTS	Library of New Testament Studies
L-N	J. P. Louw and E. A. Nida, editors, *Greek-English Lexicon of the New Testament: Based on Semantic Domains*. 2 vols. 2nd ed. New York: United Bible Societies, 1989.
LXX	Septuagint
NICNT	New International Commentary on the New Testament
NIV	New International Version
NLT	New Living Translation
NovTSup	Supplements to Novum Testamentum
NRSV	New Revised Standard Version
NTG	New Testament Guides
NTS	*New Testament Studies*
OTP	James H. Charlesworth, ed. *Old Testament Pseudepigrapha*. 2 vols. ABRL. New York: Doubleday, 1983, 1985
RevExp	*Review and Expositor*
SBJT	*The Southern Baptist Journal of Theology*
SBLMS	Society of Biblical Literature Monograph Series
SBLDS	Society of Biblical Literature Dissertation Series
SP	Sacra Pagina
SNTSMS	Society of New Testament Studies Monograph Series
TDNT	G. Kittel and G. Friedrich, eds. *Theological Dictionary of the New Testament*. Translated by G. W. Bromiley. 10 vols. Grand Rapids: Eerdmans, 1964–76
THNT	Two Horizons New Testament Commentary
TNTC	Tyndale New Testament Commentaries
TynBul	*Tyndale Bulletin*
WBC	Word Biblical Commentary
WW	*Word and World*
WUNT	Wissenschaftliche Untersuchungen zum Neuen Testament
ZNW	*Zeitschrift für die neutestamentliche Wissenschaft und die Kunde der älteren Kirche*

1 PETER COMMENTARY

INTRODUCTORY ISSUES

In this section, I highlight various positions taken on the standard introductory issues concerning 1 Peter.[1] These include discussions of authorship and date, as well as the identity of the audience and the specific situation they faced. I also address the approach taken in this commentary.

Authorship and Date

The issues of authorship and date are tightly intertwined and a decision on one of these affects the other. Many of the recent technical commentaries have espoused pseudonymous authorship of 1 Peter.[2] However, arguments for pseudonymity are, upon closer inspection, weaker than often thought. For example, the argument that the Greek of 1 Peter is too refined for a Galilean fisherman is not convincing when we consider the role of an amanuensis.[3] Another argument appeals to the numerous parallel traditions between 1 Peter and other early Christian writings.[4] Thus, Marshall, someone who is comfortable with the notion of pseudonymity (although carefully defined), claims that "if ever there was a weak case for pseudonymity, surely it is in respect to this letter."[5] The difficulty lies in how one

---

1. Much of this material is taken and summarized from du Toit 2016.
2. Achtemeier 1996: 1–43; Elliott 2008: 118–30.
3. For a discussion of the Greek of 1 Peter, see Jobes 2003: 159–73. For a discussion of the role of an amanuensis, see Richards 2004: 59–93.
4. For a recent and thorough discussion, see Williams and Horrell 2023: 1:116–62.
5. Marshall 1991: 21–22. For those favoring Petrine authorship, see Bauckham 1997: 153–66; Jobes 2005: 5–19; Green 2007b: 6–8.

conceives of authorship. Some contemporary conceptions of "authorship" may be too simple and restrictive. Evidence from the Graeco-Roman world suggests a range of understandings regarding who constitutes an author of a work. For example, Cicero states, "My poor little studies (or if you like, ours) have simply pined away from longing for you.... When [Pompey] expresses a desire to hear something of mine, I tell him that, without you, I am altogether dumb."[6] Cicero is here referring to the aid of his amanuensis. In another letter, Cicero states, "I should like you [the amanuensis] to write in my name to Basilius and to anyone else you like, even to Servilius, and say whatever you think fit."[7] The letter is still understood to be 'authored' by Cicero, even though the amanuensis has written it without direct dictation. Talbert, studying Cicero's *Letters to Atticus*, notes at least five ways Cicero refers to authorship.[8]

a. Authorship as writing in one's own hand (2.23.1)
b. Authorship as writing by dictation (4.16.1)
c. Authorship as collaboration in writing (11.5.1)
d. Authorship as authorizing someone else to write (3.1.5)
e. Authorship "as if" by the putative author (6.6).

Thus, the very notion of authorship is complicated by what we mean today in comparison to ancient understandings of authorship, and what they considered valid practice.[9] Contemporary concerns regarding authorship should not be allowed to cloud historical judgment.

With regards to Jewish thinking around the concept of authorship, Karel Van der Toorn, in *Scribal Culture and the Making of the Hebrew Bible*, has demonstrated at length that scribes played a huge role in collecting, editing, and producing ancient documents, and that it was indeed a regular practice to name a scroll after either the originator of the tradition, or the first or a major contributor to the tradition, not after the scribe who actually produced the document often decades or centuries after the tradition had first been formed.[10] He writes:

---

6. Cicero, *Fam.* 16.10.2.
7. Cicero, *Att.* 11:5.
8. Talbert 2007: 8.
9. See further Gupta 2013: 196–217.
10. See Van der Toorn 2007: 27–51.

So long as we think of the Bible in terms of authors, our understanding of its origins is bound to be impeded. In antiquity, authorship was invoked to assert authority. Those who actually manufactured texts did not see themselves as authors. They did not pursue originality, and what they wrote was not, in their eyes, an expression of talent but a manifestation of craftsmanship. They were scribes rather than authors. Moreover, the books that the scribes produced were not books in the modern sense of the term. They were not comparable either in form or function. Scribes wrote scrolls (rather than books) for the benefit of other scribes (rather than for private readers). A book market did not exist, nor were there public libraries; in fact, there was no reading public of any substance. Texts reached the people by being read out loud by someone from the literate elite. Writing and reciting were complementary facets of the scribal craft, and the Bible came into being through the agency of the scribes. Its message was proclaimed from the mouths of scribes and it was preserved for later generations through the skill and diligence of the scribes. In many respects, then, the Bible is the fruit of scribal culture.[11]

Pseudonymity need not be considered a deceitful practice nor a blatant attempt at forgery, but rather a normal practice in a culture with a deep reverence for ancient traditions which in a largely illiterate society relied on scribes to be the copiers, preservers, and presenters of the tradition in written form.[12] Inasmuch as the writers of the NT appear to have been almost entirely Jews or God-fearers deeply steeped not only in the OT but in Jewish ways of handling sacred traditions and sacred texts, we should not be surprised if 1 Peter conformed to such traditions of passing on materials.

Regarding 1 Peter, the opening, "Peter, an authoritative representative of Jesus the Messiah" (1 Pet 1:1), may indicate that Peter is the originator of these ideas that have been molded to suit the particular situation of Anatolian Christians by a later (Jewish) Christian or it may indicate the apostle Peter as the lead collaborator in the writing of this letter.[13] These options may help resolve the difficulties scholars have had in understanding the authorship of 1 Peter and should lead to a humility in our claims.[14]

11. Van der Toorn 2007: 51.
12. See Meade 1986.
13. Bauckham 1988: 469–94, has offered criteria for assessing pseudonymity and judges that 1 Peter does not conform to these criteria.
14. Throughout this commentary I use "Peter" as a reference to the person(s) who informed the composition of this letter without making any specific claims regarding the identity of said person(s).

While the discussion surrounding the date of 1 Peter have often depended on conclusions regarding the authorship, once the difficulty of the authorship problem is realized, dating this epistle becomes complex. It thus seems prudent to suggest a date for 1 Peter somewhere between 60–90 CE. Given the use of 1 Peter by 1 Clement and Polycarp, the latest date should be around the 90s CE.[15] If this text was written during the lifetime of the apostle Peter, a date around the 60s seems plausible, especially in the wake of the Neronian persecution.

Audience

Caution must be taken when trying to reconstruct a profile of the original audience.[16] However, this caution does not prevent scholars making reconstructions beyond stating that "the composition of the audience is consistent with the heterogeneity of the populations of Asia Minor in general."[17] Some have sought to offer profiles of an aspect of the audiences to whom Peter writes. Thus, Elliott has offered a sociological profile,[18] Horrell has offered an economic profile,[19] and Williams has offered a sociohistorical profile of the audience with regards to their persecution by outsiders.[20] Nearly all scholars take a position on whether the audience is predominantly Jewish or gentile, and whether the prejudice they face is official persecution or social harassment. Methodologically this presumes that the textual evidence available is sufficient for us "to discern some of the characteristics with regard to the addressees of our particular documents from what the respective authors say."[21] Although cautious, Tellbe helpfully states the following concerning the intricacies of this reconstruction.

> The text should be regarded as a vehicle, which not only constructs the self-understanding of the reader/s (individual and social identities) but which may also reflect the existing realities (both relating to the author and to the community of the addressees). It is therefore the responsibility of the exegete to reconstruct the

---

15. Elliott 2000: 135–38.
16. So Achtemeier 1996: 50; Michaels 1988: xlv.
17. Seland 2013: 45.
18. Elliott 1990.
19. Horrell 2013: 100–132.
20. Williams 2012b: 117–27.
21. Trebilco 2007: 10. See also Lieu 2004: 9.

realities in and behind the ancient text (whenever it is possible), particularly in the light of the vast amount of archaeological and inscriptional evidence at our disposal today.... We thus need to consider the fact that texts *both* potentially construct the "imaginative" or cognitive world of the readers *and* reflect in some way the social, political and religious world of their authors (and to some extent also of its readers).[22]

In this section attention will be focused on various features of the text of 1 Peter that help us to reflect on the type of audiences addressed, and the level of understanding needed to competently engage and implement the vision and instruction offered by 1 Peter.

There are several clues within the text of 1 Peter that suggest that the author is somewhat familiar with the general circumstances of these Christian communities.[23] Williams notes that, "The very existence of the epistle is proof that the author knew of Christian communities scattered across Asia Minor (1 Pet 1.1) who were experiencing persecution (1.6–7; 2.18–20; 3.13–17; 4.3–4, 12–19; 5.9)."[24] Furthermore, that Peter writes to these communities in an instructive manner, addressing slaves and free (2:16–18), wives and husbands (3:1–7), young and old (5:1–5), rich (3:3) and poor (2:18), presumes some kind of knowledge and relationship between himself and the communities addressed. The specific topics addressed (suffering, social harassment, etc.) may further indicate a knowledge of the issues affecting these Christians. Thus, Williams notes that "in order to provide his letter with the opportunity of accomplishing the purpose for which it was intended (5:12), it is natural to assume that the author had some familiarity with the readers' situation; otherwise, his response would have all-too-likely been considered superficial."[25]

There are three general options for understanding these audiences. Either they are Jews, "proselytes," or gentiles.[26] Scholars usually take none of these categories exclusively, but predominantly one of these is taken as

---

22. Tellbe 2009: 51.

23. On the extent to which the author of 1 Peter knew about the particular circumstances of the recipients, see Warden 1986: 21–50.

24. Williams 2012b: 19.

25. Williams 2012b: 20. Elliott 2000: 95, is of course right to note that our understanding of the audience "is at best inferential."

26. For example: Witherington 2008: 25–33, argues for a predominantly Jewish audience. Van Unnik 1980: 3–82, argues that they are proselytes. Van Rensburg 2009: 199–230, here, 209, suggests they are "God-fearers."

accurate with respect to the audiences addressed. It is my contention that the audience is predominantly composed of gentile converts.[27] Several reasons provide a cumulative case for this position. Firstly, it is unlikely that the Jewish Christian who authored this work would refer to his inherited Jewish traditions as *mataios* (1:18), a word associated throughout the LXX with pagan idolatry.[28] Secondly, the vices in 4:3 relate most commonly to gentile excess. Furthermore, it is highly unlikely that pagans would be "surprised" that Jews no longer joined them in their flood of unrestrained immorality (4:4). Less conclusive but still suggestive evidence is found in 1 Peter 1:14, which describes the audiences' former desires that they had in ignorance, a common Jewish description of pagans (Jer 10:25; Wis 13:1; 14:18; Gal 4:8–10; Eph 4:18). In 2:9–10, Peter describes the audience as those "called out of darkness," and those who were "once not a people." This more likely refers to pagans than to Jews. Taking these strands of evidence together strongly suggests that the audience is composed mostly of pagan converts. Although predominantly composed of former pagans, it is possible to suggest that there were also ethnically Jewish converts amongst these Christian communities.[29]

Situation

The early Christians addressed by 1 Peter find themselves scattered throughout Anatolia among the ancient areas of Pontus, Galatia, Cappadocia, Asia, and Bithynia (1 Pet 1:1). By converting to Christianity, these Christians undermined the social cohesion of relationships both inside the household and beyond. Their faithfulness to God created tensions and problems about how to negotiate life in the Graeco-Roman world. A prominent site of this tension was the household. Since the household was seen as the basic building block of society, the disruption of conventions and the dishonor caused by devotion to someone who was crucified by Roman authorities

---

27. This is the consensus view. See Elliott 2000: 94–97; Achtemeier 1996: 50–51; Horrell 2008: 48; Williams 2012b: 91–95.

28. Throughout this commentary, I use the term "pagan" in a non-pejorative sense of anyone who is not a Jew or a Christian.

29. So Mitchell 1993: 3; Elliott 1990: 65–67; 45–46 with 55–56nn76–77; McKnight 2004: 378–86, here 380. Horrell 2008: 48, notes that "converts with some prior knowledge of Judaism and its Scriptures would have been better placed to understand the letter than those without such knowledge. But aside from such generalizations it is difficult to be sure."

was deemed dangerous and threatening by many outsiders. Because of this, these Christians were suffering social harassment and perhaps even formal charges and punishment by various authorities. It is into this context of suffering social harassment that Peter wrote his letter to these Christians to help them "stand firm in the true grace of God" (5:12).

Peter frames the situation of the audience as something that is difficult, dangerous, and painful (1:6; 2:20; 3:9, 14, 17; 4:12, 14–16; 5:8–9). In 1:6, Peter describes their situation as "suffering various trials" using the word *peirasmos* (cf. 4:12). This can refer to various kinds of testing such as God's individual test of Abraham in asking him to sacrifice Isaac (Gen 22:1; Sir 44:20; 1 Macc 2:52). It can also refer to corporate testing, such as that of Israel in the wilderness (Exod 15:25; 16:4).[30] What is important for us to note here is the specific eschatological use of *peirasmos*. This refers to the extraordinary suffering, tribulation, and trial of the people of God, often termed "the messianic woes."[31] Thus Jeremias notes, "This word (*peirasmos* in Greek) does not mean the little temptations or testings of everyday life, but the final great Testing which stands at the door and will extend over the whole earth."[32] Peter understood these Christians to be experiencing a time of great testing and temptation. Since 1 Peter 5:9 states that "your brothers and sisters throughout the world are undergoing the same kinds of suffering," we may look at why Christians in the first century were suffering and compare that to the situation of 1 Peter (1 Thess 1:6; 3:3, 7; 2 Thess 1:4, 6).[33] The main cause of suffering originates from their refusal to worship gentile gods. "Christians invited persecution by their denial of the gods of Rome, which earned them the label atheists."[34] On top of this we have references to suffering (*pathēma*, 1 Pet 1:11; 4:13; 5:1, 9, and *paschō*, 2:19–21, 23; 3:14, 17–18; 4:1, 15, 19; 5:10).[35] Some of these references are to Christ,

30. For other examples, see Dubis 2002: 86–89.

31. See Wright 1992: 277–79; Allison 1985: 5–25; Pate and Kennard 2003. An eschatological understanding of *peirasmos* may be seen in Matt 6:13; Luke 11:4. It is also found with an eschatological sense in Luke 22:28–30; 1 Thess 3:3–5; 2 Pet 2:9; Rev 2:10; 3:10. For comment on some of these texts, see Dubis 2002: 90–93.

32. Jeremias 1967: 105.

33. Barclay 1993: 512–30, here 514, argues that the term *thlipsis* refers to the "social harassment" of these Christians. This situation of suffering seems comparable to that faced by the audiences addressed in 1 Peter.

34. Garnsey and Saller 1987: 174. See further Selwyn 1950: 39–50; de Ste Croix 1963: 6–38.

35. See Davids 1990: 30–44.

but they still apply to the audience because Christ is their example to follow, despite the suffering they might endure. It is precisely the suffering Christ (2:22–24) that is the model for these suffering Christians (2:21). Thus, from Peter's perspective, the situation of the audience is dire. The audience is portrayed as "powerless and without legal recourse."[36]

The kind of suffering they are experiencing is predominantly social harassment from outsiders. The question remains however, what *kind* of suffering is inflicted by outsiders.[37] Does 1 Peter indicate an official imperial sponsored persecution? Or does the situation envisaged by 1 Peter imply sporadic and localized harassment from the general populace? I am inclined to think of the situation in terms of local and sporadic social harassment from various pagan neighbors, but I cannot rule out a more official kind of persecution. Thus Holloway states, "Commentators who describe the suffering of the readers of 1 Peter as social ostracism with little or no reference to the ever-present threat of active persecution fail to do justice to the predicament facing these early Christians."[38] Bechtler states, "Although no imperial persecution is in evidence, it does appear that the local authorities considered Christianity basically criminal, with the result that some had been arrested and even condemned to death for their faith (4:15–16)."[39] He further notes, "Virtually all scholars today agree that the suffering with which 1 Peter is concerned is not due to an Empire-wide persecution of Christians instigated by the emperor; and most describe the situation in terms of social ostracism at the hands of their non-Christian neighbours."[40] Schutter rightly argues that local authorities may have acted on their own accord without official legislation against Christians.[41] Achtemeier offers a helpful overview and argues that no empire-wide persecution is envisaged, but that it is possible that local authorities were actively involved in persecution of these Christians.[42] Williams has offered a detailed analysis of the history of Petrine scholarship on this issue and notes that several scholars from the 1800s onward argued for official persecution of these Christians

---

36. Schüssler-Fiorenza 1983: 262. For a helpful imaginative sketch of the kinds of suffering likely faced by Christians in the first century, see Oakes 2001: 89–96.

37. Achtemeier 1996: 28.

38. Holloway 2009: 68.

39. Bechtler 1998: 8. See Goppelt 1993: 41–42, 58–60.

40. Bechtler 1998: 56.

41. Schutter 1989: 14–17.

42. Achtemeier 1996: 23–36.

depicted in 1 Peter.[43] Williams has further offered a detailed monograph on these issues in *Persecution in 1 Peter*, providing detailed evidence of the accusatorial nature of much of the legal system in Roman Asia Minor.[44] Williams states that any account of the situation faced by these Christians "must account for the ever-present and always looming danger of legal trials which could arise simply for adherence to the Christian faith."[45] Holloway is probably right when he states that, "Something more severe than verbal abuse is also in view in 1 Pet 4:12–19."[46] An example of such accusatorial prosecution is evident from Pliny (*Ep.* 10.96.2; 10.97.1)[47] and thus legal trials may provide the background to the *apologia* in 1 Pet 3:15.[48] But while it is probable that the social hostility experienced by these Christians at times went beyond social harassment in the form of verbal abuse, it must be admitted that from our author's perspective, the dominant portrayal of the hostility faced by these Christians is *verbal* abuse (1 Pet 2:12; 3:9, 16; 4:4, 14).[49]

The reason these Anatolian Christians are being socially harassed is due to their allegiance to Jesus (4:16) and their failure to practice cultic sacrifice to the gods (4:3).

> Association with the name of Jesus and the group spreading across the Mediterranean in his name did not make an individual popular with his or her neighbours. On the contrary, being dedicated to one and only one God, choosing a new primary reference group (namely, the church), and being committed to live out the ethical values of this God in community with fellow believers made the convert appear antisocial and even subversive. In almost every region, Christians appear to have faced their neighbour's attempts to rehabilitate them, to cajole and pressure them back into a more acceptable way of life.[50]

43. Williams 2012a: 275–92, here 277–82.
44. Williams 2012b: 131–78.
45. Williams 2012b: 331.
46. Holloway 2009: 71.
47. See Robinson 2007: 206–20.
48. Williams 2012b: 309–16.
49. Recognizing that the hostility experienced by these Christians may have been physical violence (2:20), on which see Selwyn 1964: 52–56, 91, and Williams 2012b: 301–3.
50. DeSilva 2004: 841. Mitchell 1993: 10, "In the urban setting of Pisidian Antioch where spectacular and enticing public festivals imposed conformity and a rhythm of

It is clear from 1 Peter that the social harassment they are facing is predominantly from pagan outsiders. First Peter 4:4 describes the agents of harassment and notes that this is because the Christians do not participate in the vices of 4:3, thus making it more likely that those persecuting these Christians are pagans. This likelihood is increased when we see that Peter focuses special attention on how Christians are to interact with pagan outsiders. First, we have instruction concerning pagan civic authorities (2:13–17). Second, we have instructions to Christian slaves of pagan masters (2:18–19) who are *skolios* (2:18).[51] Third, Peter instructs wives of pagan husbands (3:1–2) who cause *ptoēsis* (3:6). Because the slaves and wives are exemplary for the rest of the community, we may take this as further evidence that the source of their suffering is pagan outsiders.[52] This is further indicated by a series of texts throughout 1 Peter that suggest it is from their various networks of relationships that these Christians received criticism (2:12; 3:14–17; 4:12–17). These strands strongly suggest that those responsible for the suffering of these Christians are pagans.

The Approach of This Commentary

Sometime in the middle of the second century, we have Justin Martyr describing the response of some early Christians to the sociohistorical situation of hostility that many faced:

> Now it is obvious that no one can frighten or subdue us who believe in Jesus throughout the whole world. Although we are beheaded and crucified, and exposed to wild beasts, and chains, and flames, and every other means of torture, it is evident that we will not retract our profession of faith; the more we are persecuted, the

---

observance on a compact population, where Christians could not (if they wanted to) conceal their beliefs and activities from their fellows, it was not a change of heart that might win a Christian convert back to paganism, but the overwhelming pressure to conform imposed by the institutions of his city and the activities of his neighbours."

51. Balch 1981: 106, "The motivation for the slanders from society mentioned in 1 Peter was not that Christian slaves were politically revolutionary or that they were demanding their freedom from their masters, but simply that they had become Christians and refused to worship the traditional gods."

52. On slaves and wives being exemplary models for the Christians addressed, see Achtemeier 1996: 192, 195, 209, 217; Boring 1999: 106–7; Bauman-Martin 2004: 253–79, here 255; Elliott 1990: 206–7. Schertz 1992: 265, "These slaves and wives are, in turn, models for the community in the larger questions of the Christians' relations to the structures of human order and to the cosmic struggle of good and evil."

more do others in ever-increasing numbers embrace the faith and become worshippers of God through the name of Jesus.[53]

The scenarios faced by the Christians addressed by 1 Peter are not as dire as the situation described by Justin, but as we know from Pliny, who tortured and killed Christians for their confession of Christ (Pliny *Ep.* 10.96), the situations addressed by this letter are only going to get worse.[54] The question raised by this kind of scenario is important: How do Christians navigate and negotiate the hostility of outsiders to the Christian movement? It is my view that the entire letter of 1 Peter is addressed to this overarching question. Following Caird, I suggest that "1 Peter is written to dissuade Christians from buying immunity from persecution by making themselves at home in their pagan environment."[55] In what follows, I seek to understand this letter as an exhortation and encouragement for them to hold the line of faithfulness (1 Pet 5:12). That is the first horizon of this commentary that I shall attend to.

The second horizon I shall endeavor to attend to, is our own placement within the world as those seeking to be faithful to Jesus today. In other words, how does 1 Peter aid Christians today in navigating and negotiating life in an ever-increasing secular context that is either indifferent or hostile to the vision and values of historic Christianity? I was not born or raised in a Christian context and so when I began my journey with Jesus, my life was turned up-side down. I was raised in South Africa, just at the so-called end of apartheid. I say "so-called" because a political decision did not change attitudes and actions and I was reared in a context of white-privilege and insidious racism. Following Jesus brought me into a multicultural church that began the healing of past prejudices and the formation of someone now committed to God's restorative justice within the church.[56] I currently find myself located in a small town on the beautiful South Island of Aotearoa, New Zealand. This new context, heavily influenced by secularism, provides another fruitful context for fresh engagement with 1 Peter as I

---

53. Justin Martyr, *Dial.* 110.4.
54. See further Hartog 2014: 49–79; Kinzig 2021.
55. Caird 1994: 160.
56. I am grateful to the works of Christopher D. Marshall, a New Testament scholar who has dedicated much of his publishing career to indicating the continuities and contribution between Jesus and issues of contemporary justice. See Marshall 2001 and 2012. I am also grateful for my time working at Tearfund New Zealand, which allowed me to explore this in greater detail and to aid Christians in thinking through issues of justice in relation to the poor, the environment, and forgiveness.

seek to help Christians across denominations work out what loyalty to Jesus looks like here. Those are, broadly speaking, my contexts from which I write this commentary. Hopefully my convictions and location are more of a benefit than a deficit.

COMMENTARY

Letter Opening and Greeting (1:1–2)

¹ Peter, an authoritative representative of Jesus the Messiah: To the chosen exiles of the Diaspora in Pontus, Galatia, Cappadocia, Asia, and Bithynia, ² according to the foreknowledge of God the Father in the sanctification of the Spirit because of the obedience and bloodshed of Jesus the Messiah: Grace to you and also peace be multiplied to you.

Peter here identifies himself as an apostle, namely, a commissioned and authoritative representative of Jesus the Messiah.[1] The title "Messiah" implies the kingship or authority of Jesus. The first followers recognized Jesus as the one whom God had sent to redeem Israel, and the nations. Peter is therefore one authorized to carry forward Jesus' mission and message, and this letter is an instruction in that direction.

The recipients are identified as *the chosen exiles of the Diaspora*, an unusual description, which has almost no parallel in early Christianity. The letter of James is addressed to "the twelve tribes in the Dispersion" (1:1). But 1 Peter appears to have been written to a predominantly gentile audience. Conceptually similar terms are used in 1:17 and 2:11, where "exile" is repeated. It appears that these terms were specifically chosen because of their heritage as referents to both Israel and her heroes (Gen 23:4; Lev 25:23; 1 Chr 29:15; Pss 39:12; 119:19).[2] These metaphors function in a comparative and interactive way. They serve to compare the audience's current

---

1. Williams and Horrell 2023: 1:305.
2. However, they also have a wider source domain in Graeco-Roman culture and would thus resonate with the audience. See Elliott 1990: 24–27.

experiences of hostility and estrangement with those of both Israel and her heroes, and the estrangement experienced by their own contemporary socio-political foreigners.[3] Used as a theological metaphor it describes their elect position and distinctiveness within a pagan society.[4]

The idea of being God's *chosen* people, or his elect, is scattered throughout the Scriptures. We should however note that election is inclusive and not exclusive, as some have thought. What we mean is that election is there so that God can use people to extend blessing to everyone. The chosen are chosen to be a blessing to all (Gen 12:1–3). Israel was chosen to be the light of the world, a nation that would show others the way to God. Jesus' idea is similar in John 15:16. Election is not an exclusive relationship, but rather an *inclusive vocation*. Peter writes to Christians spread out across Asia Minor that have been chosen by God, to be his holy people in these diaspora locations. Later in 1 Peter 2:4–10, this theme will be elaborated on and developed, but for now it is sufficient for Peter to note that these Christians are not random people from the world, but rather those God has included for his purposes in the world. The notion of being "chosen" gives these people a particular sense of identity and belonging, which encourages their faithfulness to the vocation that God has called them to.

Along with being "chosen" they are further identified as "exiles," and this forms the thematic foundation for what follows throughout the letter. Their exilic status is modelled on Israel in exile, where the chosen people find themselves in a culture and context as a minority group who are vulnerable to the various social, political, and cultural forces at play.[5] Yet here the metaphor of "exile" is used to describe not their historical or spatial relocation, but rather their social and cultural dislocation from their culture and their previous lives. Through God's purposes they have become "strangers" or "aliens" to their own cultures. They have chosen to "walk in the footsteps of the Messiah" (2:21), and this has significant and often severe consequences.

The letter is addressed to those in the Diaspora in Pontus, Galatia, Cappadocia, Asia, and Bithynia. This may have formed the route that Silvanus (cf. 5:12) would have taken in delivering this letter to the scattered Christians throughout this area. But perhaps Silvanus only delivered it to

---

3. A helpful discussion is provided by Williams and Horrell 2023: 1:217–23.
4. See Achtemeier 1996: 80. See also Goppelt 1993: 67–68.
5. See Smith-Christopher 2002.

the port city in Pontus, and then someone else or others took the letter on to further destinations.

The addressees are chosen exiles according to the *foreknowledge of God the Father* (v. 2). God's foreknowledge is said to be the deciding factor in choosing people. But "foreknowledge" is quite different to what our assumptions may lead us to think. Some will be tempted to see a reference to historical theology's notion of predestination. But this seems to import too much into the text. Foreknowledge in this context does not refer to abstract information or data regarding future entities or the various realities of life. Rather, it refers to the phenomenon of *knowing* via acquaintance (Gen 18:19; Jer 1:5; Hos 13:5; Amos 3:2). For an audience that is socially afflicted and harassed, this truth is liberating and comforting. They are not forgotten strangers, but God's chosen instruments to make his glory known throughout the world (2:9–10).

The Father's divine initiative is seen in the creation of a community who find themselves in various geographical and social locations but also within the realm of the sanctifying work of the Spirit. The path to sanctification, or becoming holy, is found in direct relationship to the activity of the Spirit. Peter's vision of the Christian life originates and is directed by the inspiration and empowering of the Holy Spirit. This is pivotal for Peter's vision of what it means to be a follower of Jesus in a pagan society. Without living in the realm of the Spirit, the process of sanctification—which we will see necessitates embracing the faithful paradigm of Jesus (2:21–25)—becomes impossible to fulfill. There is no kind of Christianity where life in the Spirit is not necessary. Failure to grasp this will make Peter's vision seem unrealistic and unattainable.

All of this is possible because of the obedience and bloodshed of Jesus the Messiah. The final section of this verse involves a difficult grammatical issue that gives rise to two very different interpretations. The first offers a meaningful and pastorally suggestive interpretation. According to this view, living in the sphere of the Spirit allows one to become "*obedient to Jesus the King*," taking the Greek preposition *eis* as telic. A life in the Spirit that does not lead to obedience to Jesus is no life in the Spirit. It appears as if Peter is suggesting that the natural overflow of living in the realm of the Spirit is to live in obedience to Jesus. Nothing else corroborates our experience of the Spirit better than our lives and their conformity to the pattern of Jesus. Although this is the traditional interpretation offered by scholars, there is another interpretation.⁶ Taking the preposition *eis* as causal, this interpretation is that the chosen people of God are sanctified by the Spirit and relate to the Father and Spirit because of Jesus' fidelity, especially seen in his sacrifice. It is because of Jesus and what he has done that a life in the Spirit is possible. This makes more sense of the verse contextually and exegetically and offers Jesus as the paradigmatic model and theological foundation of life in the Spirit and faithfulness as God's chosen one, something Peter elaborates on in 2:21–25. It is furthermore on this basis that the opening prayer may be offered: Grace to you and also peace be multiplied to you. God's gracious and peaceful disposition towards these chosen exiles is based on the sacrificial offering of Jesus and the sanctifying work of the Spirit. By embracing Jesus and the salvific benefits he has provided, they are invited to live within the realm of God's sanctifying Spirit which enables them to access the grace and peace of God offered to them. This will be needed as they seek to faithfully navigate their lives in hostile areas.

---

6. See Agnew 1983: 68–73.

Praise to God the Great Benefactor (1:3–12)

First Peter 1:3–12 forms one sentence in Greek. It extols the great compassion of God and celebrates the many salvific benefits for those who call upon this God. This opening section can be divided into three categories where Peter focuses on the future and how that shapes their experience now (1:3–5), their complicated present experience (1:6–9), and then the past, which indicates their privilege of living in a time of First Testament fulfillment (1:10–12). Rather than simply being a prayer, this section sets out to announce God's compassionate activities that should be celebrated and remembered as they face their various grueling circumstances.

A Living Hope (1:3–5)

> 3 Praise to the God and Father of our Lord Jesus the Messiah because by his abundant compassion he has given us new birth into a hope that is alive through the resurrection of Jesus the Messiah from the dead, 4 and he has given us an inheritance that is imperishable, undefiled, and unfading, kept in heaven for you, 5 who are being protected by the power of God's faithfulness for a salvation ready to be revealed in the last time.

There are three prepositional phrases that indicate the result of God's compassionate intervention which creates new life for the Christian. We are born again into (a) hope, (b) an inheritance, and (c) salvation. Each one of these items is then further described by a series of adjectives. They are given a *living* hope (v. 3), an *indestructible* inheritance (v. 4), and salvation that is *already* prepared for them (v. 5). The writer also provides three specific reasons for their new reality. They have a living hope because Jesus has been raised from the dead (v. 3). Their inheritance is secure because God is faithful and powerful (v. 4). Lastly, their salvation is ready because God is actively at work on their behalf (v. 5).

This section begins with a liturgical expression "Praise to God . . . ." Blessing God is common throughout Scripture (e.g., Gen 14:20; 24:27; Exod 18:10) and has here been incorporated into an epistolary format. The liturgical purpose is there due to the function of such letters being read within early Christian gatherings (cf. Col 4:16; 1 Thess 5:27). The author will now enumerate the many reasons why the addressees should celebrate and praise God. The theocentric focus of the author is established by focusing the attention of the audience first and foremost on God, who is identified specifically as the God and father of our Lord Jesus. There were many gods in the ancient world, and the Greek word for "god" was not a proper noun, i.e., not a name of a deity. That is why there is a concerted effort throughout early Christian writings to identify the "god" being addressed and described in their writings. Amy Peeler has recently demonstrated what the Christian tradition has long known, namely, that while God is *Father*, God is not male.[1] Rather, the analogical language of "Father" indicates God's steadfast commitment, care, and concern for people.[2] The reason this God should be praised is because of his abundant compassion, often translated as "his great mercies," which celebrates the many implications of God's work identified in 1:2 for these Christians (cf. Exod 34:6). The great compassion of God leads to new life. This is a familiar notion with the God of Israel, who continually delivered and rescued Israel throughout her story of failure or infidelity. God characteristically responds with compassion to the cries of his people (e.g., Isa 30:18; 49:13; 54:10; 63:7). We should note that this was a distinctive characteristic of God when compared with Graeco-Roman understanding. Edwin Judge has noted that mercy was understood as a defect, a "disturbing emotional pathology of the soul that the rational man must learn to regulate." Mercy or compassion "was a defect of character unworthy of the wise and excusable only in those who have not yet grown up. It was an impulsive response based on ignorance."[3] In

---

1. See Peeler 2022. See also the important comments of Gregory of Nazianzus *Oration* 31.7.
2. Peeler 2022: 11.
3. Judge 2010: 185.

contrast, God is to be praised for his consistent compassion which has now become the experience of these followers of Jesus. Compassion is not passive but takes initiative to act on behalf of people who are in need.

The intervention of God's compassion (cf. 1:2, 23) has provided a new life for these Christians, indicated by the metaphor of "new birth" (cf. 1:23). The idea of "new birth" has no significant OT antecedent but the idea is found in early Christian writings (John 3:3–5; 2 Cor 5:17; Titus 3:5–6; Jas 1:18; 1 John 3:9; 5:1–4). The image of *new birth* indicates a completely new way of being that shapes their perception, relationships, community, and praxis. This results in three distinct elements, namely: (a) hope, (b) inheritance, and (c) salvation. Their hope is a "living hope" (1:3) which came to them through the "living word of God" (1:23) based on Jesus the "living stone" (2:4) who invites those who embrace him to also be "living stones" (2:5) and enables them to "live for what is right" (2:24). This is only possible because of God's great and merciful action through raising Jesus from the dead and now in giving those who follow Jesus the same living hope and salvation.

Biblical hope is not wishful thinking, but rather a confident expectation of good for the future based on the reality of God's vindicating of Christ.[4] That Jesus has been raised from the dead is the secure foundation upon which the church's hope is laid. It is this truth that secures their future inheritance and the reason it can be described as "imperishable, undefiled, and unfading" (1:4). In a world that was uncertain and too often harsh, their orientation and experience of life is hopeful because of God's victory in and through the resurrection of Jesus. The preposition *eis* is thus understood as communicating purpose.[5] That is why Peter enjoins praises to God for his great mercy. Their living hope is in God who raised Jesus from the dead, demonstrating that even death is not a match for God's power.

God's great mercy is on further display in that he has given them not only new life and hope, but also a future inheritance that is secure. Through God's work of regeneration (i.e., new birth) they are brought into a new family and thus gain a new inheritance. This inheritance is the future reward of the righteous. Whereas Israel had often acted in such a way as to forfeit their inheritance (cf. Deut 30:1–10; Jer 2:7; Lam 5:2), these Christians are offered an inheritance that is secure. The notion of an inheritance indicates that this is to be understood as a future, thus eschatological, reward.

---

4. For a contemporary reflection, see Bockmuehl 2012: 7–24.
5. Williams and Horrell 2023: 1:348.

By describing this as an inheritance, the parent-child analogy is further indicated (1:2, 17). God is their father, who provides them with a living hope that provides a secure future inheritance. It is possible to view the living hope and the inheritance as synonymous. However, I would suggest that the inheritance is something separate, the result of living with hope. The living hope is something that the Christians could experience in their tumultuous lives whereas the inheritance is something eschatological; it is something to look forward to with anticipation and excitement. Whether this is a reference to a reward, the completion of redemption, or the new heavens and earth is not noted. Perhaps it is all of these.[6]

Verse 5 begins with the reassuring promise that God is protecting them. Given what we are about to discover about the audience's situation in 1:6 and the rest of the letter, this promise is worth remembering and celebrating. Just as God is preserving their inheritance (v. 4), similarly, God is actively protecting them (note the present participle *phrouroumenos*). The final phrase, *dia pisteōs*, presents us with two interpretive options, one of which is rarely considered. Does this refer to the *fidelity of God* towards Christians or the *faith/fulness of Christians* towards God? The first thing we should note is that to distinguish too sharply between faith and faithfulness is a mistake.[7] Secondly, the focus of the passage is on giving thanks to God for what God has done, namely, acted mercifully, providing new life, hope, and a future inheritance that is secure, as well as making the promise here of protection. All these are indicators of God's faithfulness to them.[8] The ultimate act of God's faithfulness to them will be in their salvation, understood as beginning now (2:2) but culminating in being rescued from final judgment (4:17–18) and participating in "eternal glory" (5:10).

A Testing Present (1:6-9)

> **6** For that reason, you greatly rejoice, even if now for a short time you have suffered various trials **7** so that the quality of your loyalty (being of much greater value than gold that, though perishable, is tested by fire) may be found to result in praise and glory and honor when Jesus the Messiah is revealed. **8** Although you have not seen

---

6. Beare 1970: 83–84, notes that "the inheritance is untouched by death, unstained by evil, unimpaired by time; it is compounded of immortality, purity, and beauty."

7. See Bates 2017.

8. Horrell 1997: 110–15.

Jesus, you love him; and even though you do not see Jesus now, you trust him and rejoice with an indescribable and glorious joy, **9** receiving the outcome of your faithfulness, the salvation of your lives.

The phrase "for that reason" refers to the content of verses 3–5, which provide the reason for the rejoicing noted here. These Christians have been given new life and a living hope through the resurrection of Jesus from the dead (v. 3). Then, they have a future inheritance that is secure (v. 4). Furthermore, they are currently being protected by the power of God's faithfulness, which will protect them by providing a salvation at the last time. Thus, past, present, and future provide reasons for them to greatly rejoice despite their present circumstances of trials and suffering.

The word for "rejoicing" here is *agalliaō* which is found in 1 Pet 1:6, 8; 4:13.[9] Another word, *chara*, is also found at 1:8. The joy here is partly one of anticipation. As the news that a couple are expecting a child can cause people to rejoice in anticipation, so to the promise of God's eschatological salvation, allows these Christians to rejoice in their present circumstances. Furthermore, there is a measure of joy that can be experienced in the present as they experience the blessings and benefits of the new life that God has so mercifully provided.

The" tribulation," (*peirasmos*) can refer to various kinds of testing such as God's individual test of Abraham in asking him to sacrifice Isaac (Gen 22:1; Sir 44:20; 1 Macc 2:52). It can also refer to corporate testing, such as that of Israel in the wilderness (Exod 15:25; 16:4). Various texts in 1 Peter speak of eschatological salvation (1:3–4; 5:1, 4, 10) and judgment (1:17; 2:23; 4:5–6, 17–18). Yet there is interplay between the present and the future, as the present prepares disciples of Jesus for their future glory. It is within this eschatological framework that we are to understand 1 Peter's use of *peirasmos* in 1:6 and especially 4:12–19. The reason for their suffering is left unstated here (cf. 4:16), but the rest of the letter makes clear that it is caused by social and physical harassment from those who know of these Christians (2:12, 18–20; 4:3–4, 14, 16). Perhaps such harassment and opposition is instigated by demonic forces (5:8). Fidelity to God and Christ is the ultimate cause of their suffering (3:17; 4:3–4, 16).[10] God is seen as the benevolent benefactor who bestows upon them great blessings and assurance, not the one who causes them trouble and hardship just so that he can deliver them. Their trials are compared to being "tested by fire" (cf.

---

9. See also Matt 5:12; Luke 1:47; 10:21; John 5:35; 8:56; Acts 2:26; 16:34; Rev 19:7.
10. See du Toit 2021: 411–30, 421–26.

4:12, "fiery ordeal"). This indicates the severity of the tribulation they are currently facing and the need for Peter to reassure them that this will only last a "short while" (1:6) compared to their "eternal glory in Christ" (5:10).[11]

While the current situation provides a pressure test of their fidelity, they are reminded that a fidelity to Christ that survives the fire of their current circumstances is more precious than gold. In fact, it is so precious that it will result in "praise, glory, and honor." It is not entirely clear to whom this praise, glory, and honor is directed. Instinctively, we may assume that such fidelity under fire will bring ultimate praise, glory, and honor to God because they have trusted God's promises and provision and remained faithful to Christ (cf. Phil 1:11; Rev 5:12–13). However, it may be the case that Peter here envisions these Christians receiving praise, glory, and honor, from God because of their continued devotion to God despite the current sufferings faced (cf. Rom 2:7). Just as Christ is honored for his faithfulness through the cross, so too these Christians will be honored for walking in the steps of Christ and remaining faithful amidst such trying circumstances. Perhaps we are to understand this as part of the judgment scene where praise, glory, and honor are ultimately directed at God (2:12; 4:11, 13; 5:11), who then shares it with those who belong to him (cf. 4:14).

In verse 8, Peter offers a remarkable contrast by noting that although they have not seen Jesus, they maintain their love for him. It is not clear whether this "seeing" relates to the historical Jesus or to their current experience of the risen Christ. However, the appropriate response to God's lavish mercy poured out upon his people is to *rejoice*. The resurrection of Jesus, the assurance of a good inheritance, and the promise of God's fidelity to those who will be saved provides solid reasons for these Christians to maintain a hopeful and joyful disposition embodied in and through their love for Jesus. No circumstances should prevail over our rejoicing in God's acts on our behalf. The transition to verse 9 notes that another reason the addressees are currently rejoicing is because they are presently experiencing a foretaste of their salvation. That the Christians "are receiving" (note the present participle) salvation indicates that salvation *begins* in the present but is only eschatologically *completed*. The future impinges on the present in a transformative manner, allowing these Christians to experience the joy of their already-but-not-yet salvific reality. The outcome of their faithfulness is eschatological salvation, which is experienced proleptically.

---

11. The idea of fire testing and purifying is common in the Graeco-Roman world. See Seneca *De Providentia* 5.10; Pliny the Elder, *Hist. nat.* 33.19.59.

Faithfulness to Christ is future-oriented hopefulness. Because salvation is here understood as that which begins now and is completed at the eschaton, it encompasses a range of elements, including the relational and transformational, both of which are perfected in the new heavens and earth restoration, as the climax and pinnacle of God's salvific activity. Peter uses the word *psychē* not as reference to a Platonically dualist anthropology but as a reference to one's whole life (cf. 1:22; 2:11, 25; 3:20; 4:19).

A Past Fulfilled (1:10–12)

> 10 Concerning this salvation, the prophets, who prophesied of the grace that was to be yours, made careful search and inquiry, 11 inquiring about the person or time that the Spirit of the Messiah within them indicated when it testified in advance to the sufferings destined for Messiah and the subsequent glory. 12 It was revealed to them that they were not ministering to themselves but to you, in regard to the things that have now been proclaimed to you through those who brought you the gospel by the Holy Spirit sent from heaven—things into which angels desire to look!

In this section, Peter informs his Christian audiences about the future expectation of the First Testament. This is not to suggest that everything in the First Testament is just about the future, but that there are clear hopes, promises, and prophecies that relate(d) to God's future intervention and redemption that are scattered throughout the First Testament. Here, Peter highlights this aspect for his audiences to let them know that they too live with a future orientation (3–5) but also find themselves as the fulfillment of the future hopes of the First Testament prophets. From Peter's vantage point, and that of the audiences, these Christians are living out the future promises of the First Testament. The prophets engaged with God and sought to know God's future acts of salvation. This salvation, which now belongs to the audiences, has been revealed in and through Jesus (1:2, 9). Throughout the letter of 1 Peter, the author will reference passages from these Scriptures (e.g., Isa 40:6, cited in 1:24–25; Isa 28:19, cited in 2:6; Isa 53:9, cited in 2:22, etc.) to alert the readers to the benefits they now enjoy, benefits that were once future hopes and have now been fulfilled in and through Jesus. This fulfillment has implications for the Christian communities Peter is addressing. It appears likely that the thought expressed here is comparable to that of Jesus, "Truly I tell you, many prophets and righteous people longed to see what you see, but did not see it, and to hear what you hear, but did not hear it" (Matt 13:17). By reminding them that they are living out the future promises of the First Testament, it further encourages them to remain faithful despite their present struggles and to trust in God's future promises for them.

Verse 10 is related to the previous section but develops along a different line, still concerning the theme of salvation mentioned in verse 9. Some scholars have questioned which era of prophets Peter refers to: First Testament or New Testament prophets? Selwyn is a rare example of one who argued that this referred to New Testament prophets.[12] That these prophets "testified in advance" seems to indicate that this is best taken as a reference to First Testament expectation. The prophets sensed God was planning something, and the vision that God had given them required careful reflection and research into the Scriptures they had access to. They knew God's grace was to be revealed, but exactly how this would work out and what it would look like was unknown to them. As they "searched and inquired" (1:11), the Spirit revealed to them various mysteries concerning the time the Messiah would come. That the Spirit is here identified as the "Spirit of Christ" indicates, as in 1:20, that Christ is viewed as pre-existent. "The Messiah whose Spirit spoke through prophets earlier has now been revealed as Jesus, the Messiah/Christ (1:19–20) who himself was 'foreknown before the foundation of the world' (1:20)."[13]

The "subsequent glory" probably refers to the resurrection, and thus the vindication by God of Jesus, revealing who Jesus is and was, and what he has accomplished for the reconstituted people of God. The prophets of the Hebrew Scriptures were helping those of this epoch to see and understand the divine intervention of God. As Cranfield notes, "The men of the Old Testament had lived with their attention turned to the future, in expectation of God's promised salvation of His people. Eagerly they scanned the far horizon, looking for the fulfilment of God's promises and their hopes."[14]

Peter argues in these verses that *Scripture* serves a "Christo-telic" function: "Scripture is seen as pointing to Christ or having Christ as its goal or fulfilment."[15] The often-used phrase "according to the Scripture" did not mean that a writer could find a few biblical proof texts that predicted

12. Selwyn 1964: 133–38.
13. Elliott 2000: 346.
14. Cranfield 1954: 28.
15. Witherington 2008: 87.

an event if he hunted hard enough. It meant that the entire biblical narrative had at last reached its climax, its appointed and God-ordained goal, in these astonishing events concerning Jesus the Messiah and the outpouring of the Spirit.[16] The Hebrew Scripture's eschatological hopes and dreams had been met and accounted for in the Messiah, and now in the messianic community. God has been faithful to the earlier prophecies, and he has delivered on his great promise to provide salvation. "In effect, this constitutes a claim that the true subject of biblical prophecy—and, by extension, of the Jewish Scriptures as a whole—is Christ, and that the fulfilment of what is said by the prophets is found in the Christian gospel and is appropriated by Christian believers."[17]

Missionaries moving through the areas mentioned in 1:1 are said to have announced this great news to those in the regions of Pontus, Galatia, Cappadocia, Asia, and Bithynia. Peter thus sets a paradigm for missionary activity as actively going to places where the gospel has not been proclaimed. Christians are not to run and hide themselves from the rest of the world, but rather to engage in the mission of God. We may only speculate where these missionaries came from, but we can infer that Peter's apostolic ministry had something to do with this situation. Perhaps what we find here is similar to the Pauline situation with the Christian community in Colossae, where Paul had not specifically planted the local church there but still retained apostolic oversight and input into the Christian gathering. Perhaps Peter had sent missionary envoys into these parts to actively proclaim the gospel, and through these missionaries, he established networks of communities who had responded to the gospel.

They did this *by the Holy Spirit*, suggesting that the Spirit is the initiator of gospel proclamation. Marshall helpfully points out that "the Spirit who inspired the prophets also inspired the evangelists and gave them insight into the true meaning of the prophets."[18] It is the Spirit that aids proclamation concerning Jesus, just as it was the Spirit that aided the prophets of old as they searched and enquired about God's great salvific achievement. Williams and Horrell suggest that it is the Spirit who is offering proclamation through the missionaries.[19] And the community must continue to look to the work of the Spirit in their efforts to announce this colossal saving event

16. Wright 1992: 400.
17. Horrell 2008: 62–63.
18. Marshall 1991: 47.
19. Williams and Horrell 2023: 1:445.

that God has accomplished. The Spirit is said to be "sent" from heaven, indicating the divine origin of the message proclaimed.[20] This would suggest that the Spirit is the divine representative of God who executes God's will and advances God's mission. Just as Peter is an *apostle of Jesus the Messiah*, so too the Spirit is representing God's will and mission. The same Spirit that was operative in and through the Old Testament prophets is still operative now amongst the saints of God in the New Testament era. And, as Marshall notes, "What the prophets foretold is now the content of the evangelistic message of the church."[21]

The prophets longed to see what God would do, angels too desire to investigate, and possibly understand, this great salvation that has come upon us. Luke 15:10 provides a possible analogy where the angels of heaven rejoice over the sinner being reconciled. These Christians whom Peter addresses are in the privileged position of living in the time of great fulfillment. The angels, who are not omniscient (Mark 13:32; Rom 16:25–26), have been waiting to see when and how these prophetic hopes would be fulfilled, and now they have been.

We are left with the question as to why Peter has authored this pericope? Part of the reason must be to demonstrate that the mission of God that these followers of Jesus are currently involved in is part of God's mission throughout history. Peter's vision allows us to suggest that his intentions are to communicate that the Hebrew prophets of old still play a vital role in the current mission because they were "serving" not themselves but those to come afterwards. The First Testament played a vital role in sustaining and guiding the understanding and praxis of these Christian communities, and we would be wise to follow their example.[22]

This passage alerts the audience that they are living within the time of fulfillment. Things into which angels longed to look have now come to pass. These Christians are living at a climactic moment in God's unfolding drama of salvation and have a key part to play, just as the prophets of old played their key roles in searching the Scriptures. The OT is not just a time-bound book. It contains a record of God's promises and fulfillments. These provide fuel for faithfulness as they demonstrate and describe God's

---

20. Witherington 2008: 84, suggests that the Spirit be understood as "the chief apostle, the messenger of God's good news about Jesus."

21. Marshall 1991: 46.

22. Rosner 2013.

covenant-commitment to his people. The OT prophets lived with a future orientation, which has been radically fulfilled in the coming of Jesus.

Fusing the Horizon

Many lives have been characterized by uncertainty and confusion over the last few years. Perhaps that is nothing new, but the level of anxiety has certainly increased. A global pandemic, wars, food shortages, and the uncertainty of what comes next have all led to a greater apprehensiveness about life in the so-called modern world. In some respects, Peter's world was not that different. The early Christians scattered through Anatolia faced these same issues. And the early Christians faced the persistent threat of retaliation from those outside the Christian community. And yet, if these three sections of chapter 1 are true, then we have reason not only to have *hope*, but also to rejoice amidst the difficulties of life we currently face. There are two aspects of joy that can help us here. Firstly, there is the joy of *anticipation*, as in the announcement of someone being pregnant. Secondly, there is the joy of *actualization*, the moment that the baby is born. As Christians we constantly straddle these two elements, anticipating God's intervention and being aware of it. We live in the hope of the second coming in which anticipation will be swallowed by the actualization of God's cosmic salvation.

Yet, there should be no facile dismissal of the fact that what people are currently experiencing is difficult and at times treacherous. But such trying circumstances can be placed within a larger picture of God's relentless fidelity and sovereign power to ultimately prevail. The Christian hope is that because even death was not the end of Jesus' story, it will not be the end of ours. We can have a confident hope, a hope centered on the character of God displayed throughout the pages of Scripture. The story of Scripture is that God time and time again rescues, redeems, and restores his people, and that provides reassurance for the future. We may celebrate our eucharistic gatherings by remembering the past actions of God's faithfulness, and taking solace in the present that God will continue to act mercifully on our behalf, no matter how dire the circumstances. And even though sickness and death may seemingly prevail, those who trust in the resurrection of Jesus can anticipate a different conclusion to our stories, both individually and cosmically.

HOLY LIVING FOR A HOLY GOD (1:13—2:10)

Be Holy Because God Is Holy (1:13-16)

> **13** For this reason, keep your minds ready and exercise sober judgment, focus your hope completely on the grace that comes with the revelation of Jesus Christ. **14** Like obedient children, do not be shaped by the desires that you formerly had in ignorance. **15** Rather, because God who called you is holy, you must also be holy in everything you do; **16** for it is written, "You shall be holy, because I am holy."

Verse 13 operates as a transition verse, bringing the doxology of 3-12 to a closing climax of action and then introducing the next section. The opening "For this reason" links what follows with what Peter has described in verses 3-12. "The thanksgiving section [1:3-12] is not a formality, but a substantial liturgical-theological unit that lays the theological foundations for the practical instruction to follow. This section that may seem on first reading to be so religiously abstract is intended to provide the basis and essence of practical Christian life in society."[1] Because of God's great mercy (his initiative in our salvation, his mighty act of deliverance through the death and resurrection of Jesus), because God has been faithful to his plan, and now because we are his people, brought into his family by the Spirit, there must be a firm and concrete response from us.

Their expectation is to be *fully* (*teleiōs*) centered and focused on the grace that Jesus provides, in the present but also eschatologically, as the

---

1. Boring 1999: 60.

verse echoes 1:7.² Thinking about the future revelation of Jesus the Messiah, and his grace that will be revealed, motivates and inspires these followers of Jesus facing terrible circumstances in the present. Hope for the grace to be revealed, affects their lives now. Their present way of life, or ethics if you will, are eschatologically informed. Peter elaborates on their response to the grace already revealed when he instructs his readers to be ready, mentally, for action.

The phrase "prepare your minds" stems from an idiomatic expression from ancient times.³ To prepare one's mind involves disciplining ones' self in the ways that Peter has outlined through this letter, but which here are eschatologically framed. They are to evaluate "the present in light of its eternal significance."⁴ The word used here for "discipline" has an interesting etymology, originally indicating "sobriety" (cf. 4:7; 5:8). What Peter is suggesting is an awareness of their hope, the grace that Jesus provides, and the way this affects their lives. Unlike those intoxicated and therefore unable to act thoughtfully, followers of Jesus are to be sober-minded and carefully consider their various actions, attitudes, and relationships. Peter elaborates on what this entails through this epistle which exhorts them to rely on God's grace (cf. 5:12).

Peter refers to the audience as "obedient children," which rhetorically would encourage them to question whether or not this is how they are living and thus to make the necessary changes.⁵ This also clarifies their identity. Because God is the Father (1:2, 3, 17) they are God's sons and daughters. Children are expected to reflect their parents, follow their instructions, and implement their desires until they are old enough to make their own choices, and even then, it is hoped that children will still reflect their parents (adopting a godly character that reflects their heavenly Father).

---

2. Keener 2023: 93.

3. The Greek phrase is: *anazōsamenoi tas osphyas*, which is similar to the LXX translation of Exodus 12:11. See Jobes 2005: 111, for details. The NRSV of Exodus 12:11 reads, "This is how you shall eat it: your loins girded, your sandals on your feet, and your staff in your hand; and you shall eat it hurriedly. It is the Passover of the Lord." Luke 12:35–36: "Be dressed for action and have your lamps lit; be like those who are waiting for their master to return from the wedding banquet, so that they may open the door for him as soon as he comes and knocks."

4. Keener 2023: 92.

5. Is there a christological echo here alluding to the obedience of Jesus in 1:2? Just as Jesus was obedient, they too are to be obedient to the Father.

Since God is their Father, their lives are to reflect his character and concerns. Peter begins this call to mental action and self-controlled living (v. 13) by stating it negatively as not being conformed to the impulses and cravings that shaped their lives before they encountered Jesus the King (cf. Rom 12:2). To "be shaped" (*syschēmatizō*) is to be molded in various ways to a pre-set pattern.[6] Peter is wanting them to be conformed to God's character and have God's concerns since they are "obedient children" (cf. 1:15). But there are external forces and powers at work (1:18; 5:8), and their own previous pagan lifestyles and current pagan context (4:3–4) contribute to their present struggles. Since identity informs praxis, they are to "be who they are," namely, God's obedient children. They are not to be influenced by other determining factors, no matter what their status or position, since their new life is as children of God. Their "desires" are to be reordered in light of the revelation of Jesus the Messiah. In fact, Jesus is their primary paradigm of obedience (2:21–25), and thus they have an embodied example provided by the one to whom they are to be obedient.

Their former period of life is labelled *ignorant*, not in a negative or derogatory sense, but in the sense that they held no knowledge of Jesus and were unaware of who he was and what he had provided for them.[7] Now, however, they live in the knowledge of who their true Father is, God, and who their true Lord is, Jesus. Ignorance has passed, and they have been liberated into a new life of faith, hope, and love. Therefore, everything about them and their lives changes in the light of this revelation.

Contrasting (*alla*, "rather") their status and vocation with what they were before their conversion, Peter continues his instruction concerning both their new identity and vocation. Instead of slipping back into an old way of life, which they had in their ignorant state (cf. 1:18), they must imitate the Holy One.[8] "To be holy means that Christians must conform their thinking and behaviour to God's character."[9] The issue of holiness should not be abstracted from its direct context as the result of missionary engagement (1:12) in a pagan environment. The Leviticus codes were established, in part, to delineate Israel from other nations. They established

---

6. BDAG 979.

7. This strongly suggests a predominantly gentile, rather than Jewish, audience. Cf. Acts 17:30; Gal 4:8–9; Eph 4:18; 1 Thess 4:5.

8. Pss 70:22; 77:41; 88:19; Isa 1:4; 5:16; 12:6; 14:27; 17:7; 29:23; 30:12, 15; 40:25; 45:11; 55:5.

9. Jobes 2005: 112.

the distinctive characteristics of the people of God. They were boundary markers that notified their pagan neighbors that they were indeed different. The quotation from Leviticus 19:2 recalls the entire section dealing with various aspects of what it means to be the holy people of God. Green superbly notes:

> As Leviticus 19 has it, holiness extends indeed into the nooks and crannies of life: family and community respect (vv. 3, 32), religious loyalty (vv. 3–8, 12, 26–31), economic relationships (vv. 9–10), workers' rights (v. 13), social compassion (v. 14), judicial integrity (v. 15), neighbourly attitudes and conduct (vv. 11, 16–18), distinctiveness (v. 19), sexual integrity (vv. 20–22, 29), exclusion of the idolatrous and occult (vv. 4, 26–31), racial equality (vv. 33–34), and commercial honesty (vv. 35–36). This is a holiness of engagement, not of withdrawal.[10]

Their calling as the people of God is to be embodied in their holy conduct which marks their collective and individual identity as the children of God and is the social boundary demarcating them from pagan outsiders and from their own former past in all its ignorance. The account of holiness that Peter describes as normative for the Christian communities is shaped and influenced in a myriad of important ways by the moral vision of Israel's Scriptures. What constitutes "holiness" in 1 Peter will be shaped by the ethical framework of Israel's Scriptures and the specific pattern offered by Christ the Lord (2:21).

Excursus: Holiness and Separation

For many Second Temple Jewish writers, a connection between holiness and separation was evident.[11] Holiness entailed separation from sin, and this was ubiquitous among the pagans, and thus they should, as far as possible, sever connections between them. Thus, Jubilees 22:16–18 states: "Separate yourself from the gentiles, and do not eat with them, and do not perform deeds like theirs. And do not become associates of theirs. Because their deeds are defiled, and all their ways are contaminated, and despicable, and abominable.

---

10. Green 2007b: 44.

11. The aim here is not to demonstrate the commonality of such movements within Second Temple Judaism, but merely to note that they existed and this may have provided an influence on the author of 1 Peter.

They slaughter their sacrifices to the dead, and to the demons they bow down. And they eat in tombs. And all their deeds are worthless and vain."[12] This text is illustrative of an attitude we find among the texts from Qumran (1QS 5.1, 10–13, 15–20; 7.24–25; 8.11; CD 6.14–15).[13] Thus Swanson notes that holiness "is the assumed background of the rise of the sectarian movements of the second century BCE."[14] As holiness is a prominent theme in 1 Peter (1:12, 15–16; 2:5, 9; 3:5), this raises the question of what such holiness entails, and how one is to accomplish the calling to be holy. More specifically, does it involve separation from society, a withdrawal from the contamination of pagan culture? Does it encourage separation of Christians from pagans,[15] or is it an ethical quality, characteristic of those who imitate God (1:15–16)? Our aim here is not to explore all the facets of holiness in 1 Peter, but rather to seek an answer to the specific question of whether or not holiness entails separation from pagans.[16] The primary call to holiness is found in the instruction to imitate God (1:16, quoting Lev 19:2). But this statement raises questions about how the audience is to be holy like God, for the implications are not self-evident. The instructions in 1:15–16 elaborate positively how the audience is to fulfill the negative command in 1:14. Thus, referring to 1:14, Achtemeier correctly argues that the exhortation to non-conformity to previous ignorant desires is what become holy means in 1 Peter 1:15.[17] This is further clarified by the author as he specifically states that it is *en pasē anastrophē* that they are to *become* holy (1:15). This suggests a transformed and differentiated way of living.[18]

This perspective is most likely because the section of 1:13–21 is focused on the outworking and ethical response (cf. the inferential conjunction *dio* in 1:13) to what the author has noted and described about God's future (1:3–5), present (1:6–9), and past (1:10–12) work on their behalf. They are called "children of obedience" (1:14), who do not conform to ignorant desires. They are reminded that God is the impartial judge who will assess their work (*ergon*)

---

12. For a pagan perspective, see Juvenal, *Sat.* 14.104–5; Tacitus, *Hist.* 5.5.

13. Cf. also 1QH 2.18–19; 1 QpHab 11.13.

14. Swanson 2007: 19–39, here, 20. See further Hengel 1981: 228; Brower 2005: 21–42.

15. As suggested by Elliott 1990: 119.

16. See the discussion of 1 Peter in Wells 2000: 208–40, and Green 2007a: 311–25, which explores more of the intricate facets of holiness in 1 Peter.

17. Achtemeier 1996: 120.

18. Elliott 2000: 361.

(1:17). Further in 1:18, they are again reminded that they were *liberated* (*lytroomai*) from *meaningless ways of life* (*mataios anastrophe*). This gives the whole section an ethical focus which describes their *new life* (*anagennaō* 1:3, 22), which they now live out "in Babylon" and "in Christ" (5:13–14). Rather than separating from society, they are to exercise *sobriety* and a *mental vigilance* (1:13) towards temptations around them, and not give in to ignorant desires (1:14; cf. 2:11). The call to holiness in 1:15–16 is couched between this instruction and that which calls for conduct that conforms with the knowledge of the fear of God during their current exilic state (1:17).[19] They live as strangers and aliens in a state of exile, because of their sanctification by the Spirit and the elective call of God (1:2, 15–16). This is outworked in 3:2, where the women are exhorted to lives that are characterized by *hagnos*, using a word related to *holiness*.[20] If 1 Peter understood the concept of holiness as requiring separation from pagans, then it would not make sense to counsel women married to pagan husbands to let their husbands carefully observe the *reverence of your lives* (*hagnēn anastrophē*).[21] Rather, we would expect that they would be instructed to separate from their pagan spouses, something this author explicitly rejects in his instructions that they fulfill their duty to their own husbands (3:1).

This is why Peter refers to their honorable conduct "among the pagans" (*en tois ethnesin*, 2:12). Their identity has changed so that Peter does not consider them merely gentiles but rather those who are the people of God and part of God's household.[22] Thus Green suggests understanding holiness as a matter of living "different," or "distinctive," lives "in the midst of the Gentiles (for example, 2:9–12)."[23] Holiness in 1 Peter does not entail a geographical relocation or isolation from pagan relationships.[24] Rather these various descriptions and elements elaborate on the understanding and implications of a *holy* life set within the sphere of their former lives (1:17). We cannot abstract Peter's statements from either the immediate literary context of 1:13—2:3, or the letter as a whole, which wrestles with the *tension* of holy living in a pagan

---

19. Green 2007a: 322.
20. See L-N 88.28. The words *hagnos* and *hagios* are semantically related.
21. A similar exhortation is given to believing spouses in 1 Corinthians 7:12–16, although with more detailed instruction.
22. Forbes 2014: 75.
23. Green 2007a: 316.
24. See Green 2007a: 314; Wells 2000: 223.

world.[25] So, when Peter refers to them as a "holy priesthood" (2:5) and a "holy nation" (2:9), we should not understand this in a separatist manner, but rather that they are set apart for the purposes of God, having been transformed (1:22), so that they may now fulfill the calling of God upon them as a *holy* community (1:2; cf. Exod 19:6; 23:22; Deut 7:6–13; Wis 17:2), a *distinctive* community that reflects and represents the character and concerns of God (1:15–16).

There are two reasons to suggest that 1 Peter did not understand holiness as separation. Firstly, holiness is understood by 1 Peter as a quality of conduct and character that reflects God (1:16), and that is quite different to separation. Secondly, 1 Peter uses holiness language to describe the lives of those who are living under the watchful eye of pagans (2:12; 3:2, 5), thus negating the idea of separation. Green is correct to state that Peter "does not counsel separation from the world, as though the demands of holiness might necessarily or even possibly be parlayed into patterns of isolation."[26] Therefore, despite some groups within Second Temple Judaism holding to the view that holiness entailed separation, 1 Peter opposed such an understanding and offered the view of holiness as a transformed and distinctive way of life shaped by the character of God and the presence of the Holy Spirit, patterned on the life of Jesus.

Fusing the Horizon

To be a follower of Jesus is to commit one's self to the sanctifying work of the Spirit so that we more and more reflect God's character. We cannot do all the things that God does, nor should we try. But we are called to reflect the character of God in every facet of our lives. This assumes of course that we know what God is like. So, the journey of Christian formation begins with growing in our understanding and appreciation of the character of God revealed in Scripture. This comports well with God's created intentions for us to be image-bearers (Gen 1:27). While scholars debate the various elements of what it means to

---

25. A tension acknowledged by Elliott 1990: 108 and Balch 1986: 79–101, 81. The question is of course how to resolve this tension.

26. Green 2007a: 323.

bear God's image, it certainly includes an ongoing reflection to the rest of creation of God's concerns, cares, and commitments.[27] Thus, to be holy is to continue in our vocation to be God's representatives.

It is important then that we realize that holiness is an essential aspect of what it means to be a follower of Jesus and not some optional extra. Peter's words here are in the imperative—they are not a suggestion or an opinion but rather an *instruction* to those who follow Jesus. Secondly, living a life characterized by God's character and instructions will prove counter-cultural, as it did in the first century. "A community which reflects the life of Jesus will be a community of *generosity* and *sharing*, of *friendship* and *belonging*, of *mission* and *identity*, of *freedom* and *risk-taking*. As such it cannot but help stand out against the deeply held values of Western culture."[28] We should not therefore be surprised when those who live within the influence and direction of another worldview react negatively towards Christians who seek to live holy lives. This is because, thirdly, holiness for Christians is not a private matter but a holistic and comprehensive reordering of our priorities and commitments so that they reflect Christ in every sphere of life. Integrity demands that there is a consistency between our private and public lives, which includes all forms of digital and social media. This is because, fourthly, holiness is communal and not just individual. The life of holiness invites and necessitates communal accountability, examples, and encouragement as followers of Jesus seek to live in faithful obedience to God and his distinctive calling.

The Impartial Judge (1:17-21)

> 17 Because you call upon the Father who judges everyone without prejudice, according to each person's deeds, you must conduct yourselves reverently in this time of exile. 18 You know that you were liberated from meaningless ways of life inherited from your ancestors, not with perishable things like silver or gold, 19 but with the worthy blood of the Messiah, as a lamb without fault or flaw. 20 The Messiah was foreknown before the creation of the world but was revealed at the end of the ages for your sake. 21 Through him

---

27. See Imes 2023.
28. Riddell 1998: 69.

you have come to trust in God, who raised him from the dead and gave him glory, so that your trust and hope are set on God.

The opening Greek phrase *kai ei* should not be understood as a condition (*"If* you call") since the author is addressing Christians and there is no doubt about their relationship with God. I have translated it as "because," for it provides the reason for the following imperative (1:17b) to live a certain way. The phrase, "to call upon the name of the Lord" originally designated approaching God in cultic sacrifice and invoking him using his name (e.g., Gen 12:7–8; Ps 116:4, 17). It is used as an insider description in Joel 2:32, "everyone who calls on the name of the LORD shall be saved." It is interesting that Peter here substitutes "the Father" for "the name of the LORD" or "the name," but this is common among early Christian practice (Rom 8:15; Gal 4:6), following the teaching (Matt 6:9) and example (Mark 14:36) of Jesus. "The emphatic position of [*patera*] calls attention to the contrast between God as benevolent Father and as impartial judge of the world."[29] Impartiality in judges was a common motif among ancient writers, one celebrated in both the Graeco-Roman and Jewish world.[30] However, we should note that there is a distinctive feature of Judeo-Christian notions of partiality in the Graeco-Roman world. The God of the Bible favors what Wolterstorff refers to as "the quartet of the vulnerable": "This is what the LORD Almighty said: Administer true justice; show mercy and compassion to one another. Do not oppress the widow or the fatherless, the foreigner or the poor" (Zech 7:9–10a).[31] God's impartial justice, and the execution of such by him as judge, not only includes the vulnerable and forgotten, it seems God particularly favors those whom normal societies seem to neglect or, worse, oppress. So, Deuteronomy 24:17, "You shall not deprive a resident alien or an orphan of justice; you shall not take a widow's garment in pledge." Deuteronomy 27:19, "'Cursed be anyone who deprives the alien, the orphan, and the widow of justice.' All the people shall say, 'Amen!'" Isaiah 1:17, "Seek justice, rescue the oppressed, defend the orphan, plead for the widow." The First Testament abounds with exhortations to remember, and thus take responsibility for, those who are disadvantaged or vulnerable. These Christians to whom Peter writes should be comforted and challenged

---

29. Achtemeier 1996: 124.

30. See Keener 2023: 99–100 for details.

31. Wolterstorff 2008: 75. "A striking feature of how the Old Testament writers talk about justice is the frequency with which they connect justice, both primary and rectifying, with the treatment of widows, orphans, resident aliens, and the poor."

by the notion that the Father God they call upon will judge each of them, and everyone else, without prejudice or favoritism. This forms the basis for his instruction for them to live reverently in this time of exile, where they are socially harassed and mocked for their fidelity to Christ.

Furthermore, they are reminded (1:18-19) that they have been liberated from their past meaningless ways of life. The word "liberated" (*lytroomai*) carries the connotation of "ransom," a price paid to set someone free. By implication, Peter understands that they were thus held captive to pagan customs and religion which kept them hostage to a meaningless life. The Graeco-Roman gods were ultimately "useless" (LXX Lev 17:7; Jer 8:19; 10:15). This way of life was characterized by desires (1:14) that were shaped and informed by ignorance, which embodied a way of life that "wages war against life" (2:11) as God intended it. The adjective *mataios*, conveys the sense of "useless" or "vain." It is also used of the futility of worshipping idols (Acts 14:15). This is coupled with the word *patroparadotos*, which generally refers to ancestral traditions being handed down. Such ancestral traditions include religious traditions concerning the gods.[32] Thus, I have translated this as a reference to a "meaningless way of life" because it is disconnected from the Christian God, concerned with pagan idolatry, and that from which these gentile Christians have been liberated. Salvation is here conceived of as a liberation from problems and powers associated with a life estranged from God. Theologically, it refers to the absurdity of life without Jesus. From this state of existence, Jesus has liberated us. We should also note that 1:17 provides the positive aspect of liberation. They have been liberated not only from a futile existence offered by Graeco-Roman idolatry, but have been incorporated into God's family, with God as the Father of all. Liberation from a futile existence is also into a reverent way of life, knowing that God is the just judge who pays attention to every aspect of what they do. They live under the constant awareness of God's love and commitment, but also of God's unprejudiced judgment. This should cause them to live appropriately, reverently, as they face their daily tasks and struggles.

The focus in 1:20 then moves to the precious life ("blood") of the Messiah, which is compared to that of a sacrificial lamb. Such a lamb is required to be without fault or flaw. There is discussion among scholars about whether this indicates that Isaiah 53:7 is the background context within which to understand this passage.[33] Achtemeier prefers to understand this

---

32. See the discussion in du Toit 2021: 418-21.

33. That this passage is cited again at 2:22-24 makes this suggestion more likely. See further Elliott 2000: 374-75.

with reference to "the general sacrificial cult practiced by Israel, in which all animals were expected to be perfect; if they were not, they were unacceptable to God."[34] The perfect life of Jesus is capable of liberating us from a life of corruption and decay, so that they may live reverent and grateful lives in response to God's gracious gift of Christ. Peter here describes the notion that "the Messiah," Jesus, was intimately known from or before the creation of space and time. This *foreknowledge* implies the pre-existence of the Messiah, since he was foreknown before the foundation of the world. This is a christologically significant aspect of Jesus' messiahship as understood by Peter.[35] Peter wants his audience to realize that the revelation of the Messiah was no accident of circumstance but was orchestrated before the founding of time itself. God knew that it would take a divine representative, the Messiah in this case, to reveal to his people who God was. This messianic figure would also deliver God's people and restore them to a right relationship with God, due to his obedience and victories. Thus, it was "for their sake." As Green states: "Building on the undeveloped but assumed premise of Christ's pre-existence, Peter urges that God's own agenda and initiative stand behind Jesus' redemptive work. To put it differently, the sacrificial death of Jesus must be taken seriously as providing insight into the very nature of God."[36] Peter's eschatology comes to the fore here as he announced that God's colossal saving act, in and through the Messiah, has been revealed at a climactic stage in his unfolding purposes. The coming of Jesus was for the salvific benefit of the audiences addressed (1:21). This was God's intention all along. Furthermore, the author insists that Jesus is the agent through whom people gain access to and relationship with God. That they have come to trust the God who raised Jesus from the dead indicates that their lives are oriented around faithfulness to God in the light of God's gracious benefaction of salvation towards them and the accompanying loyalty that God has towards his people. Just as Jesus was vindicated by God through the resurrection, and thus given glory, this provides the foundation for their own trust and hope in God, so that they too may be raised and restored. Eschatology thus shapes their everyday lives and encourages them to live in the hope and trust that God's judgment will not fail but will vindicate them and further liberate them from the social struggles they face.

---

34. Achtemeier 1996: 129.
35. See also Keener 2023: 109.
36. Green 2007b: 37.

Fusing the Horizon

In the epic movie *Gladiator*, Maximus Decimus Meridius in a charging speech to his soldiers reminds them that "Everything we do in this life echoes in eternity." So too everything we do as Christians will be assessed by God. That is a sobering thought. But not one that should paralyze us in guilt or fear, but rather one that should motivate us to embrace God's cause and concerns, and to live reverently and distinctively as God's people, knowing that God judges without prejudice. Chris Tilling once said, "Naïve faith can mean a life not lived in accord with the kingdom of God."[37] And here we have instruction from Peter that reminds us of God's loving omniscience and holy character that each of us must face. While knowing that God is intimately aware of every single detail of our lives may be an overwhelming thought, it is meant as an encouragement, not a threat. As Brooke wisely notes, "The accusations of conscience are stilled in the presence of omniscient holiness, which is perfect love."[38] The Father's commitment to us should allay any lingering shame or regret so long as we bring them to his forgiving and transforming attention and care. God has provided a salvation for us in Christ so that we have opportunities before the great judgment to rectify our mistakes, and with those whom we have hurt or grieved. As we remember the lamb who was slain on our behalf, we must remember that we are those who have been redeemed. We are those who are able to approach the throne of grace because we trust in a God who cares deeply (5:7) and whose love can cover over a multitude of sins (cf. 4:8).

New Life, New Family, Same Gospel (1:22–25)

> 22 Having detoxed your lives by your obedience to the truth so that you have authentic mutual love, love one another deeply from the heart. 23 You have been born anew, not of perishable but of imperishable seed, through the living and enduring word of God. 24 For "All flesh is like grass and all its glory like the flower of grass. The

---

37. Private correspondence.
38. Brooke 1912: 98.

grass withers, and the flower falls, **25** but the message of the Lord endures forever." That message is the gospel that was proclaimed to you.

The gospel has had a transformative effect on these gentile Christians. Peter's response here is insightful yet peculiar. It appears that he is suggesting that obedience to the truth is the means by which one rids oneself of the toxic elements in this world. The perfect tense of the participle "having purified" (*hēgnikotes*) suggests that the audience is currently in a state of purity. But this raises the question of whether this refers to entrance into the Christian community at conversion or an ongoing process of sanctification as one embodies obedience.[39] We should perhaps not differentiate too strongly between such options as the process begun at conversion is maintained through continual obedience. Obedience is not understood to be an optional extra but as an integral aspect of our discipleship. We are "children of obedience" (1:14) who embrace the way of life revealed through the obedience of Jesus (1:2; 2:21). The *truth* may refer to the gospel of Jesus and what he has done, and therefore what that means for his followers at conversion. But Peter's letter is a reminder and exhortation to continue in this truth (cf. 5:12). The teaching of the previous section suggests that 1:13–21 may provide a suitable guide to an aspect of the truth that Peter has in mind. The fact that Jesus is the one through whom God may be known appears to be the central feature of which Peter speaks. By implementing Jesus' lordship in their daily lives, by practicing his holiness and living out his example, their lives are purified from the continued dark effects of a culture and society estranged from God, just as it was at conversion.[40]

Living the truth creates and sustains a community of followers that are to care for one another. "It is the reality created by that obedience that now makes the next step in Christian life possible, namely, the wholehearted love of the other members of the Christian community."[41] Peter exhorts them in their current state of purity to therefore engage in acts of purity, namely *love for one another*. The goal of purity is mutual and familial love for one another. This is not just any kind of love, but a love that is deeply concerned for the wellbeing of others. There is no genuine Christian life without a concerted and committed care for sisters and brothers in Christ.

---

39. See the discussion of Williams and Horrell 2023: 1:540–44.

40. Thus, we follow Achtemeier 1996: 136n13 in suggesting that "the ἐν has its force as an instrument of means."

41. Achtemeier 1996: 136.

One cannot be a faithful Christian without being involved in the Christian community. Life in Christian community is a space where one continues to purify one's life through continued obedience to the truth, with the goal of performing informed and transformed acts of love for one another.

The theological rationale for authentic mutual love is found in conversion, where Christians are given new life "through the living and enduring word of God." This is another secure reality, like their inheritance (1:4). As Green notes, "'new birth' is a dramatic metaphor for a decisive transformation of life."[42] The word of God begins to shape and transform those who have entered the new life that God has provided.

In contrast to the transitory and fragile world, which is perishing, Isaiah 40:6-8 proclaims that God's word and work endure forever. The beautiful world with its glory will ultimately fail. All humans are mortal and will pass away. Since these Christians have been given new life through an imperishable seed, they will not experience ultimate decay, but "after you have suffered for a little while, the God of all grace, who has called you to his eternal glory in Christ, will himself restore, support, strengthen, and establish you" (5:10). The verse encourages an eschatological perspective on their temporal situation. As new creations with new life, they are to shape themselves with what will last and not with what will fade away. Isaiah's message is a gift from the past that illustrates the point well. The First Testament prophets longed to see and experience what these gentile Christians have in and through the gospel (2:3). This proclamation from Isaiah has now come to them and been fulfilled among them. Isaiah's gospel has been prophesied and proclaimed (1:10-12) among these gentile Christians. It has also been embraced and embodied as they seek to be holy (1:15-16) and obedient (1:14, 22). The "word" that was proclaimed to Israel is the same "word" that is proclaimed to this gentile audience. Thus, there is continuity between the people of God in the Hebrew Scriptures and the people of God in Christ.

New Covenant Asceticism (2:1–3)

> 1 Therefore, remove all depravity, and all deceit, hypocrisy, envy, and all evil speech. 2 Like newborns, long for the reasonable, pure milk, so that by it you may grow into salvation—3 if indeed you have recognized that the Lord is kind.

---

42. Green 2007b: 49.

While this section forms a distinct unit, it carries forward the discussion of 1:22–25 by describing first negatively (2:1) and then positively (2:2–3) how the community may live together in "obedience to the truth" with "genuine mutual love" (1:22). By avoiding the vices in 2:1 they are shown negatively how they may further "grow into salvation" (2:2). Having felt the impact of the word of God in their lives (1:23–25), the great news about Jesus and what he has done, Peter now notes the consequences of an encounter with Jesus (1:22; 2:1). Holistic moral transformation is in view here. There are dark activities that destroy relationships, damage God's people, and undermine the witness of God's people (cf. 2:11–12). Therefore, they are to be done away with. Peter envisions the continued removal of such destructive behaviors from the fabric of our lives. The word *apotithēmi* is usually connected with taking off garments (2 Macc 8:35; Acts 7:58; Josephus, *Ant.* 8.266; Mart. Pol. 13.2), but it is also used in various lists as a reference to the elimination of evil deeds (Rom 13:12–13; Eph 4:25–32; Col 3:8; Jas 1:21; cf. Heb 12:1; 1 Clem 13.1). The use of "all" is familiar in vice lists (Eph 4:31; Col 3:8; Jas 1:21; 1 Clem 13.1), and suggests a comprehensive action of removing *everything* that contaminates the life of Christians seeking to be reflective of God's character and concerns. What kinds of dark materials have we clothed ourselves with that Peter instructs us to put aside? What I have translated as "depravity" (*kakian*; cf. 2:16) could be understood as "evil behavior" (NLT), "ill will" (CEB), or "malice" (NRSV). This is part of a recurring theme in 1 Peter concerning *evil deeds* (2:12, 14–16; 3:9–12, 17; 4:15). The translation *wickedness* also comes close to its semantic range. The word "deceit" (*dolos*) refers to those "taking advantage through craft and underhanded methods."[43] As part of vice catalogues, it appears here and in Mark 7:22; Rom 1:29; Did. 5.1; Barn. 20.1.[44] Next, the NRSV opts for the translation of "insincerity," while the NLT suggests "hypocrisy." It is connected to the notion of play-acting or pretending, but with a negative taint.[45] The community of Christians are to be those "without hypocrisy" in 1:22.[46] Envy is described by Aristotle as "a disturbing pain excited by

---

43. BDAG 256.

44. For other early Christian uses, see Matt 26:4; Mark 14:1; John 1:47; Acts 13:10; 2 Cor 12:16; 1 Thess 2:3; 1 Clem. 16.10; 22.3; 35.5; 50.6; Ignatius, *Eph.* 7.1; *Pol.* 8.1.

45. Giesen 1990: 3:403.

46. It is used in Wis 5:18; 18:15; Rom 12:9; 2 Cor 6:6; 1 Tim 1:5; 2 Tim 1:5; Jas 3:17; 1 Pet 1:22.

the prosperity of others."⁴⁷ It is always described as a vice, and it is noted how it destroys *harmony*, something Peter commends in 3:8.⁴⁸ Evil-speech "probably refers to habitual disparagement of others rather than some kind of openly slanderous speech."⁴⁹ This theme occurs several times in Peter's narrative (2:12, 15; 3:16; cf. 3:9–10).⁵⁰ Jesus is given as an example of someone who does not engage in a riposte of verbal abuse towards those who persecuted him (2:23). We should not imagine such an instruction to have been easy, but it is what they have been called to in Christ.

Depravity, deceit, hypocrisy, envy, and evil-speech are all garments of darkness that are to be removed by the community since its members are part of a community of purity and mutual love (1:22), having implemented—and continuing to implement—the truth. "Taken together, they represent the kind of attitudes and actions in whose presence true community based on love is impossible, and that are therefore absent among those who have heeded the command to love one another."⁵¹ Peter urges them to focus their attention elsewhere by changing the metaphor from garments of destruction (2:1) to young children who need their mother's special provision. Having been born anew into a living hope from the living word, they are now to live new lives conformed to the character of God (1:15–16) and the way of Jesus (2:21). To what does "milk" here refer? Jobes argues for "God's life-sustaining grace in Christ" and thus not a reference to Scripture or "the word" of God.⁵² Other scholars suggest that the referent here is to the "word of God" (cf. 1:23). However, if we allow 1 Peter 5:12 its place, it appears plausible to suggest that *the word of God* always gives witness to *the life-sustaining grace of God*. Therefore, these two interpretations need not be mutually exclusive. "Christians are thus to yearn for the undiluted word

---

47. Aristotle, *Rhet.* 1386b18–19. "Envy is pain felt at deserved good fortune, while the feeling of the malicious man has itself no name, but such a man shows his nature by rejoicing over undeserved ill fortune. Between them is the man inclined to righteous indignation, the name given by the ancients to pain felt at either good or bad fortune if undeserved, or to joy felt at them if deserved." Aristotle, *Eth. eud.* 1233b20–26.

48. See T. Sim. 4:8. Dio Chrysostom, *Oration* 77/78, outlines the way envy can lead to the destruction of relationships and even violence.

49. Achtemeier 1996: 144.

50. Other early Christian references include: 2 Cor 12:20; 1 Clem. 30.1, 3; 35.5; Barn. 20.2; Pol. 2.2; 4.3; Herm. Man. 2.1.2–3; 8.1.3; Herm. Sim. 9.15.3; 23.2–3.

51. Achtemeier 1996: 145.

52. See Jobes 2005: 131–41.

of God with the same tenacity with which an infant yearns for its milk."⁵³ An encounter with the grace of God, revealed through the word of God, naturally causes growth in Christians as they are sustained by the grace of God. Whether this refers to eschatological deliverance or spiritual maturity is unclear. Adapting language from LXX Ps 33:9 [Ps 34:8], the author reasons that because they have experienced the goodness and loyalty of God, this provides the theological justification for ridding themselves of toxic attitudes and behaviors (2:1) and embracing the nourishment provided by God so that they can grow into their salvation (2:2). Their awareness of God has been beneficial and has led them to a place where they "love" God (1:8) and are grateful for the salvation that they have begun to experience, even rejoicing in that salvation as they await its future consummation (1:6).

A New Covenant Community (2:4–10)

> ⁴ Come to him, a stone that is living. While rejected by people, he is chosen and precious in God's sight. ⁵ As living stones yourselves, be built into the Spirit's household, to be a holy priesthood, to offer spiritual offerings acceptable to God through Jesus the Messiah. ⁶ The Scriptures state: "Look, I am placing a stone in Zion, a cornerstone that is chosen and precious; and whoever trusts in him will not be ashamed." ⁷ So for those who trust in him, he is precious; but for those who refuse to trust, "The stone that the builders rejected has become the cornerstone," ⁸ and "a stone that makes them blunder, and a rock that makes them fall." They stumble because they disobey the word, as they were supposed to. ⁹ But you are an elected race, a royal priesthood, a distinctive nation, God's own people, in order that you may proclaim the mighty acts of him who called you out of darkness into his marvelous light. ¹⁰ Once upon a time you were not God's people, but now you are God's people; once upon a time you had not received God's mercy, but now you have received God's mercy.

Peter shifts metaphors here from that of spiritual growth (2:1–3) to that of a building and building materials. There is a strong emphasis on the corporate nature of the people of God throughout this passage. The section provides an intricate scriptural meditation on the identity and experience of Christ and the identity and experience of the people of God. Key similarities between Christ and the people of God are highlighted, as

---

53. Achtemeier 1996: 147.

well as God's response to the plight of both Christ and the christological community, i.e., the church. There are a series of contrasts that are noted throughout this section: rejection and election; shame and honor; and trust and denunciation.

Having "tasted that the Lord is good" (2:3), people are now coming to *him*, namely, Jesus. Interpreters struggle with the syntax of verses 4–5. Is this a rhetorical device seeking the audience's active participation in God's building project ("Come to him . . .") or is he describing the audience's incorporation into the people of God through the agency of God ("as you come to him . . .")? It is likely that this section is indicative and that God is to be understood as the agent who is building his community on the foundation of Christ, the cornerstone (v. 5).[54] As people entrust themselves to Christ and so are joined to the Christian community, they are "being built" (2:5) into a *spiritual* household, namely, a community characterized by the work of the Spirit. This spiritual community is built upon the foundational cornerstone of Jesus, who is described as "a living stone." The first part of this image references an important theme in 1 Peter, that of *living*. There is a "living hope" (1:3); "the living and enduring word" (1:23); "live for righteousness" (2:24); God will "judge the living . . ." (4:5); and the Christians are called to "live in the Spirit" (4:6). The participle "living" when used attributively with "stone" refers to Christ as the one who is alive, as opposed to the ubiquitous idols that parade the landscape of the ancient world. There may be an implicit contrast to the "futile ways inherited from your ancestors" (1:18) with their dead idols.[55] The First Testament is replete with references to idols made of "stone" (Deut 4:28; 28:36, 64; 29:17; 2 Kgs 19:18; Isa 37:19; Jer 2:27; 3:9). And while God is also metaphorically described as a "rock" (Deut 32:4; 2 Sam 23:3; Isa 26:4; 30:29; Pss 1:3; 18:2; 19:14; 62:3), here Peter carefully refers to Christ as a "living stone"—not one who is lifeless and thus useless, but rather one who is reliable, alive, and involved with the affairs of humanity. Like the spiritual nourishment of 2:3, here in 2:4 Christ is not only the life-giving savior (1:3) but also the life-sustaining one to whom they must come and be joined together with others for their individual and corporate benefit. The stone metaphor is pursued in verses 4–8. The second section is concerned with the people of God, which picks up this idea from verse 5.

---

54. See Dubis 2010: 47–48.
55. See du Toit 2021: 411–30.

It may be difficult to understand, but this living stone, this life-giving Savior who offers hope and mercy, has been rejected by those outside the Christian community (vv. 7–8). Those who have rejected Christ are not just those who crucified him, but those who are now rejecting Christ in the proclamation of the gospel by these Christians. We know this from the use of the present participle "disobey" in verse 8. When Peter writes of Christ, he does so in an exemplary manner for the pastoral benefit of his audiences. Just as they are experiencing rejection, so too Christ also continues to experience rejection.

The notion of being "rejected" and the contrast with that being "chosen" and "honored" reminds us of their identity as "chosen exiles" in 1:2 and sets up the identity markers in 2:9. Christians live in the tension of being honored and rejected at the same time, just as Christ is. Contrary to the human judgment of Jesus, God's perspective is significantly different. Christ is the elect and the honored. Jesus is the one "who has ascended into heaven and is at the right hand of God, with angels, authorities, and powers made subject to him" (3:22). Jesus' mission and message, life and death, have been vindicated by God. This is pastorally relevant to the community that is currently facing rejection and harassment. They too will ultimately be vindicated by God. Despite the shame they are currently experiencing from outsiders, God, the ultimate arbiter of what is good and honorable, will honor them. As Boring rightly notes:

> Their new status remains a nonstatus in the eyes of the world; their security is neither visible to empirical observation nor a matter of the heart. It is not found in "feeling good about themselves" and "having a sense of self-worth," but is a turning away from themselves and finding the meaning of their lives in their incorporation into God's saving plan for history and the elect and holy people of God.[56]

The notion of a "spiritual house/household" is the segue from the architectural metaphor to the image of the people of God as the new temple.[57] "It is a 'spiritual house' in that the Spirit forms it and especially in that it is not physical. . . . The house of God is no longer to be thought of as a physical building, but as a living 'house' in which God lives."[58] The purpose for

---

56. Boring 1999: 98.

57. Cf. Mark 14:58; 15:29; John 2:19; 1 Cor 3:16–17; 6:19; 2 Cor 6:16; Eph 2:19–22; 1 Tim 3:15; Heb 3:6; 10:21; 12:18–24; Rev 3:12; 11:1. So Michaels 1988: 100.

58. Davids 1990: 87.

which God is building his Spirit-filled household is so that they can be a holy priesthood (cf. 1:15-16; 2:9). Peter's purpose here is not to argue that each individual is a priest and so should function in that manner. Elliott rejects the idea that this "spiritual house" should be understood as God's temple.[59] But the vocabulary of "holy priesthood," "spiritual sacrifices," and "cornerstone" are highly suggestive.[60] Thus, the purpose here is to identify the community of Christians as God's temple who function as a priestly community that is called to perform various priestly functions, such as offering spiritual sacrifices and giving witness to the virtuous acts of God (2:9-10), who has redeemed the community through his relentless merciful activity.

Given the strong emphasis on holiness within this letter, it is best to take the phrase "spiritual sacrifices" as a comprehensive reference to every facet of Christian life that reflects the character and concerns of God and moves within the trajectory of the example set by Jesus.[61] Sacrifices that are acceptable to God are christologically shaped and determined. The example and teachings of Jesus are the filter for determining what is holy and acceptable to God (1:15-16; 2:21). Marshall is right to note that such sacrifices are not to atone for sins.[62] Rather, as with the First Testament's various types of offerings, such sacrifices are a response of gratitude to God for his great act of redemption in and through Christ (1:3-12, 18-19). Our lives are to be offered in Christ as a testimony of gratitude to God for the "precious life of Christ" (1:19).

Alluding to Isaiah 28:16 in verse 6, Peter picks up on themes begun in 2:4 but inverts them. Here he deals first with Christ, the living Stone who is to be understood as the cornerstone that has been chosen and honored by God.[63] This will be followed by two quotations, one from the Psalms and another from Isaiah, regarding the stone's rejection. The introductory formula, "for it states in Scripture," applies to both quotations in 1 Peter 2:6-7, and perhaps the allusion to Isaiah in 2:8.[64] Woan notes that, "In the

59. Elliott 1966: 153.
60. Keener 2023: 129.
61. Bauckham 1997: 153-66, here 163, "Since the description in 2.5 anticipates 2.9-10, the 'spiritual sacrifices' are best understood as the whole way of life which, as God's holy people, they are called to lead, and by which they proclaim his mighty acts to the Gentiles."
62. Marshall 1991: 69.
63. For a discussion of the image of the stone, see Hillyer 1971: 58-81.
64. Woan 2004: 217.

context of 1 Peter it is clear that the author has seen the [Lord] of the psalm as Christ. No explanation, argument or apology is given for this; it is natural and self-evident for the author and his church."[65] There are two basic responses to Jesus. "The 'stone' in their way is either a foundation stone to which they can commit themselves without any concern over being let down, or it is the 'stone' that, due to their rejection and God's eventual exaltation, leads to their fall."[66] To those who embrace Jesus, he becomes precious to them (v. 7). This can only be understood if the consequences of the gospel are outlined. They were rescued from an ignorant and empty way of life, they were rescued from futile ways of thinking, destructive immorality, and now they have encountered the one who has cleansed their lives and incorporated them into the people of God, called to be distinctive. For those who reject the gospel, the consequences are devastating.[67] In rejecting the great news of Jesus, who he is and what he has accomplished for humanity, people reject the most significant building block in constructing their lives. The life they build is on shaky foundations with no stability, since the most important element in building has been forsaken (cf. Matt 7:24–27).

Reading the NRSV of verse 8, leads one to ask: Does this refer to a predestining to judgment? As our translation above makes clear, the subject of what is being "destined" is open. Firstly, were those who rejected the word destined to believe the word but then, due to disobedience, they have rejected it? Or were they destined to reject the word, and now through disobedience, this came to pass? Such metaphysical questions are an imposition on the thought world of our author. Secondly, we must also question, who are the "they" that stumble? Gentiles, Jews, or both? And what causes their destiny to be such? With Selwyn, we should note that "it is not stated here that this rejection is final and irretrievable."[68] One's destiny hangs in the balance of one's allegiance. As soon as one is obedient to the word, which changes one's allegiance to Jesus, one's destiny will change. Then, if the translation above is correct, God has destined them to believe the word, not disbelieve it. They were destined to believe, but through disobedience God's salvific purposes are being frustrated. People are actively rejecting

---

65. Woan 2004: 222.

66. Davids 1990: 90.

67. The phenomenon of some rejecting the gospel assumes that there is ongoing proclamation of the great news of Jesus' saving activity. This is consistent with 2:9 and Peter's emphasis on gospel proclamation throughout this epistle. Cf. 1:2, 25b; 2:9; 3:1–2, 15.

68. Selwyn 1964: 165.

God's grace, not just avoiding it, but willfully walking away from it. Another interpretive suggestion notes that this does not entail that certain individuals or groups were appointed to disbelief, but that God's decree is that those who do not believe will stumble and fall.[69] Whichever option we choose, it seems unlikely that Peter is suggesting that God has predestined people to disbelieve the gospel.

Unlike those who stumble and disobey the word, this is a community that has been transformed by the word (1:23), which has been given new life (1:3) and is being built into a spiritual house (v. 5). Here in verses 9–10, we have a kind of crescendo to this passage, which began with the story of Christ and his rejection, then moved to the identity of the Christian community and now their proclamation of the virtues of God. In 2:9, Peter accentuates the church as the bearer of the divine presence where the community of faith is incorporated as "living stones" to form a "spiritual house" in Christ.[70]

"But you" declares the contrast between those who reject the cornerstone, Jesus, with the audience to whom Peter is writing. Because of their "new birth," which is their embracing of Jesus as Messiah and Lord, they are different. What follows is Peter's elaboration on their different identity and distinctive vocation.

Using four descriptive titles, usually reserved for the people of Israel (cf. Exod 19:5–6; Isa 43:19–21), Peter writes them into the narrative of God's people.[71] He depicts them as a "chosen race," due to their trust and allegiance to Jesus (cf. 1:1, "chosen exiles"). The word *genos* implies a common origin.[72] Unlike the nation of Israel, where one was born into the nation, here faith is the determining factor. "Here, in contrast to Isaiah and Exodus, it is *faith* rather than a biological bloodline that determines inclusion in the 'elect stock' of God and that unites the elect people with their elect Lord."[73] They may have been born in Pontus, Galatia, Cappadocia, Asia, or Bithynia, and thus have prior social, biological, and geographical identity markers, but Peter claims them as united into God's chosen

---

69. Elliott 2000: 434.

70. Christensen 2018: 352.

71. Williams and Horrell 2023: 1:686 rightly follow Goppelt 1993: 147–51 in noting firstly that Peter does not address the concerns and questions we often ask concerning the relationship of Israel to the church. Peter's focus is elsewhere, namely on the relationship of the church to the world.

72. See Achtemeier 1996: 163–64. Cf. *gennaō*.

73. Elliott 2000: 435.

nation. It is perhaps why some early Christians thought of themselves as a "third race" (Diogn. 1; Tertullian, *Ad Nat.* 1.8; Clement of Alexandria, *Strom.* 6.5.41).

As a chosen race they have a special role in God's unfolding purposes, thus they are the "King's priesthood," there to perform acts of worship and sacrifice to the true and living King. Contemporary questions about whether this entails every Christian being a priest is not the concern of this passage. The focus is on the community. An important function of a priest, likely intended here, is to be a representative to God on behalf of the people and also to be a representative of God to the people. Thus, priests act as mediators between God and humanity.[74] Furthermore, together they constitute a "distinctive nation." The word *ethnos* refers to "a body of persons united by kinship, culture, and common traditions."[75] The adjective "holy" used here describes their particular identity as a nation composed of those called to a vocation and life of holiness, so I have offered the translation "distinctive." They are a nation because of the transformative word (1:23) which has given them new life (1:3) with God as their Father (1:17), who has united them into a family (2:17; 5:9) called to embrace the customs of holiness as a distinctive way of life (1:15–16; 2:21). "In the context of 1 Pet 2:9, in any case, *ethnos hagion* identifies the believers not as a politically constituted 'nation' or state but rather as a *holy people* sharing a common historical, cultural, and religious heritage."[76]

Lastly, their lineages may stem from the geographical areas of "Pontus, Galatia, Cappadocia, Asia, and Bithynia" (1:1), but their superordinate identity is as God's very own people. They were scattered among the nations, but they belong to God. Since they have been purchased, liberated, redeemed, and restored (5:10) to relationship with their creator (1:18–19), they are his own possession.

The purpose of identifying and describing God's people is "in order that you may publicly declare." Those identified as God's people have a particular purpose, which flows from their identity as God's people. Their responsibility as God's people is to be what they are, outlined in first half of verse 9, and to declare the activity and identity of the God they worship. The content of their public acclamation is "the praiseworthy deeds of God" (2:9). "The phrase itself expresses the wonder of the convert at

---

74. Duke 2003: 646.
75. BDAG 276.
76. Elliott 2000: 438.

being illumined by God and brought into his presence, which forms the emotional motive for praise and proclamation."[77] Scholars have offered a variety of ways to understand the elements of such a public proclamation. Some suggest it refers to publicly preaching the mighty deeds of God to the world.[78] Others take this as a reference to corporate worship.[79] It is not clear to me why a choice needs to be made. Psalm 118 provides a good example of declaring the wondrous deeds of God in assemblies of worship. The context of conversion in 2:9–10 and ethical witness in 2:12, suggests a missional impetus be included in our understanding. First Peter 3:15 connects the ideas of worship and mission, and perhaps scholars wanting specificity have missed something that Peter has joined together.

These Christians have been "called out of darkness." Darkness in Scripture is often a metaphor for ignorance or sin (cf. Prov 2:13).[80] Calling is an important theme in 1 Peter (1:15; 2:9, 21; 3:9; 5:10) and here refers to their invitation to not only belong but to participate in the praises and purposes of God. This is what it means to be called "into his wonderful light." "Light, created by God, is a symbol of God, a synonym for glory (*doxa*), and an image of divine salvation and deliverance (Ezek 43:2; Isa 9:1; 60:1; Acts 9:3)."[81] Thus, their conversion entails forsaking an old way of life of ignorance and sin (cf. 1:18–19) and being incorporated into a people who know God and live under the direction of God's revelatory light (cf. Ps 119:105). This is similar to what we find in the words of Jesus who calls Paul to go to the pagans "to open their eyes so that they may turn from darkness to light and from the power of Satan to God, so that they may receive forgiveness of sins and a place among those who are sanctified by faith in me" (Acts 26:18). The corporate dimension of their conversion is stressed in verse 10. Alluding to Hosea 2:23, we have a past and present comparison. At one point in their past, they did not belong to God's people, but now, due to their "new birth" (1:3, 23), they have become God's people. The defining change agent here is God's mercy. Those who have been incorporated into the people of God have responded faithfully to God's act of deliverance and blessing in providing salvation through Christ. God's mercy indicates that

---

77. Davids 1990: 93.
78. Elliott 1966: 42–43; Goppelt 1993: 151.
79. Balch 1981: 133.
80. Achtemeier 1963: 439–49.
81. Elliott 2000: 441.

God is willfully compassionate and acts for the well-being and benefit of people.

Fusing the Horizon

Walking into a multi-cultural church in South Africa in 1995, as someone who had not begun to follow Jesus at that time, was like stepping into the Twilight Zone, an alternative reality that shocked and unsettled me. I had never experienced people from different races, cultures, and socioeconomic contexts embrace one another as sisters and brothers. They freely shared the love of Christ in such a clear and embodied manner. My deep-rooted prejudices surfaced swiftly. I could not believe my eyes. This was one of my many stumbling blocks that God would deal with as he drew me closer. And the means of drawing me closer was found in this odd community of ordinary followers of Jesus attempting to live out his vision for humanity. They were lovely. Their kindness and commitment deconstructed my prejudices one by one and replaced them with a sense of awe at the transforming work of Christ. They were not perfect by any stretch of the imagination, but their hearts were committed to the cause of Christ, and they loved outsiders like me. To this day, I am so grateful that there are communities of people who are deeply committed to the way of Christ in forming and maintaining communities of difference.

In this passage Peter highlights the theological identity of the people of God, which is a superordinate identity; it takes precedence over all other identities which are to find their place in right relationship to Christ. There were likely many races and groups with different social and economic statuses among these Christian communities.[82] And now, because they had tasted and seen that the Lord is good (2:3), they had been incorporated into a new community where they were sisters and brothers, not rivals and enemies. A testimony to this is provided by Justin Martyr: "Then we hated one another and murdered one another, and, because of custom, would not even live under the same roof as those who were not of the same race. Now, after the appearing of Christ, we eat at the same table, and we pray for our enemies, and try to persuade those who unjustly hate" (*1 Apol.* 14:3). It is the mission of the church to call those trapped in darkness into the light and healing of communities that joyfully live under the superordinate identity we have in Christ. We

---

82. See Horrell 2009: 176–202.

must never allow race, culture, or social and economic differences to divide or destroy communities of faith. We must work towards the reconciling vision we have in this passage, and the one before it (2:1–3), of forsaking all depravity, deceit, hypocrisy, envy, and destructive speech. Instead, we must work towards being communities where we recognize the Lord is kind and embrace that kindness so that these stumbling blocks are overcome and the family of God can further exhibit the mercies of God.

Negotiating Life Honorably Among the Pagans (2:11—3:12)

Negotiating Life with Honorable Conduct (2:11-12)

> ¹¹ Beloved, I urge you as aliens and exiles to refrain from the carnal desires that wage war against life. ¹² Conduct yourselves honorably among the pagans, in order that, even when they slander you as evildoers, they may observe your honorable deeds and glorify God when he comes to judge.

This is a crucial passage, which encapsulates key themes that the letter addresses. The opening address of "Beloved" serves a dual function to identify the participants in the community as those whom God loves, but also those whom other members of God's family love. This marker indicates the start of the two main sections of this letter (2:11—4:11 and 4:12—5:11). A key truth that will sustain them as they navigate and negotiate life in the Graeco-Roman world is that they are loved by God and others in the church.

The word "alien" (*paroikos*) indicates someone who is not a full citizen, thus lacking the privileges and duties of other citizens. The terms "aliens and exiles" have aroused much discussion as to what exactly they mean when referring to scattered believers throughout Asia minor in imperial Rome. Does this literally mean that they were "foreign nationals," or is Peter using this as a metaphor for their current status? While it seems likely that there were actual foreign nationals among these early Christians (2:18–20), it also seems to be a most appropriate metaphor for the current status of

Christians in the empire. This language is indicative of a status of those that do not quite belong to the Graeco-Roman world they inhabit.

An "exile" (*parepidēmos*) refers to someone who is a temporary resident with no significant status. Peter uses the metaphors to describe the reality of these gentile Christians who do not fully belong to their own former cultures but are rather temporary residents in this current world, awaiting the redemption by God of all things. This brought about shame for these Christians but honor from God (4:16). This is not about their true home being in heaven, but rather about their current social situation as Christians within the Graeco-Roman world. The contrast between a positive aspect ("beloved") of their identity and then a challenging aspect ("aliens and exiles") mirrors the opening reference to them as "chosen exiles." This is the tension they must navigate daily.

As those with a new identity in relationship to God and other Christians, they are first exhorted to *abstain* and then exhorted to *honorable conduct*. The first exhortation to abstain from carnal desires is illustrated throughout the letter by the lists of vices that are not conducive to holiness or communal flourishing. The vices listed in 2:1, 4:3, and 4:15 illustrate the types of activities and attitudes to avoid. As noted, they are to practice a type of ethical asceticism, a way of life that abstains from vice. They cannot therefore simply assimilate into their culture; they are to remain distinctive, reflecting the character and concerns of God (1:15–16). A life characterized by vice is destructive to the life that God intends. *Psyche* refers to a person's whole life, not to some type of Platonic entity or ghost "like Casper" inside of an individual. A vicious way of life wages war against the way of life that God has brought about for these Christians. Peter's purpose here is to remind them of their exiled status, due to their allegiance to Jesus, which entails not getting caught in the web of carnal cravings that could eventually damage and destroy relationships within the community, and ultimately with God (3:7; 4:7). They are to "avoid" such elements since this is incongruent with their new vocation and identity as God's chosen people (1:13–18).

The alternative to a life that is characterized by vice is one that is conducted with honor. Peter employs a word readily recognizable from Graeco-Roman discourse.[1] The high frequency of this term in 1 Peter (1:15, 17, 18; 2:12; 3:1–2, 16) is suggestive that this is an important concept on which the strategy and intention of Peter hinge. Given the matrix within which to

---

1. Spicq 1994: 1:112–13.

understand this term, and that it is specifically conduct that is honorable "among the pagans" (*en tois ethnesin*), we suggest that this is conduct that is consistent with their holy calling (1:15–16) and that this refers to conduct that general society will be impressed with and applaud (2:13–14). There is an overlap in understanding what is good and beneficial. Peter does not offer us a dualistic worldview where only Christians are considered good and everyone else is understood to be evil. Rather, there are aspects of life in the ancient world that they can affirm and agree to. There are other aspects they must refrain from, such as the vices mentioned, as well as the behaviors noted in 1 Peter 4:3.

The reason for the need for their honorable conduct is that their allegiance to Jesus inevitably led to hostile responses from those outside the Christian communities. Peter takes it for granted that they will experience hostility from fellow gentiles. Their absence from cultic worship, their avoidance of idolatry, and the cultural non-conformity all but guarantee a negative response from pagans. Rather than withdraw into isolated communities, such as Qumran, these Christians are exhorted to acts that are considered honorable in the public domain. This is a significant element of Peter's strategy to neutralize hostility with others, by demonstrating honorable conduct. And to further Peter's missional commitments, by winning people over through ethical witness (cf. 3:1–2).[2]

There is significant discussion about whether we should understand the accusation of these Christians as "evildoers" as social or criminal, i.e., was it against the law to be a Christian? While there was no empire-wide law against being a Christian, there are enough hints throughout the church's first century to indicate that governments did not appreciate the existence of Christians and at times killed them.[3] Given the large geographical areas 1 Peter is addressed to, it seems unlikely that the author here thought of these Christians being accused of being criminals. However, considering the positive portrayal of governing authorities (2:13–14) and the call to honor the emperor (2:17), we cannot discount the idea that some pagans may have accused these Christians of being criminals (4:15).

Peter employs *epopteuō* twice, specifically in connection with the ethical witness of the Christians (2:12; 3:1–2) before a watching world. BDAG suggests a meaning of, "to pay close attention to, watch, observe, see."[4] The

---

2. See further, du Toit 2019: 221–43.
3. Nero and Pliny are but two examples. See Kinzig 2021.
4. BDAG 387.

present active participle suggests careful observation over a period and not a one-off glance. The character and conduct of Christians are to inspire and incite careful reflection from outsiders on the values and priorities that are embodied in their Christian lives. Or as Jesus said, "let your light shine before others, so that they may see your good works and give glory to your Father in heaven" (Matt 5:16). This careful observation of Christians and their good deeds should hopefully lead to the unbelievers glorifying God. The "day of visitation" clearly suggests an eschatological scene where unbelievers stand before God in realization of who these Christians are and what they were seeking to accomplish.

Excursus: Mission and Ethics

In contrast to the clarity of 3:1–2, there is discussion regarding the relationship between ethics and mission in 2:12 due to the ambiguous reference "glorify God when he comes to judge" (*doxasōsin ton theon en hēmera episkopēs*). Some scholars suggest that "the epiphany is God's revelation of the Gospel when preached and accepted (cf. 1.12)."[5] Others see a reference to the final day of judgment.[6] Because the "Day of the Lord" is a common concept in Jewish eschatology,[7] Achtemeier is correct to note that this probably does refer to the eschatological judgment, but wrong to suggest that this robs the passage of its missional force.[8] One of the determining factors in this discussion is whether we take the phrase *ek tōn kalōn ergōn* as causal or as a partitive construction.[9] Dubis suggests that the partitive construction is out of place here and does not fit with the supposed underlying tradition of Matthew 5:16.[10] But Dubis does not tell us why the partitive construction is out of place.[11] Furthermore, it seems likely that the Jesus tradition of Matthew

---

5. Winter 1988: 87–103, here 102n43. See also Brandt 1953: 10–25, here 17; Beare 1970: 138; Elliott 2000: 471.

6. Goppelt 1993: 160; Michaels 1988: 119–20; Achtemeier 1996: 178n83.

7. See Elliott 2000: 470–71.

8. Achtemeier 1996: 178n83. Visitation may perhaps refer to God's activity in present salvation; see Elliott 2000: 471.

9. See the discussion in Dubis 2010: 63–64.

10. Dubis 2010: 63.

11. Best 1970: 95–113, 112, reckons 2:12 "almost certainly depends on" Matthew 5:16. If that is the case, it supports the missional interpretation offered here.

5:16 is the source of 2:12, but we must inquire if there are any internal reasons within 1 Peter to suggest that 2:12 is related to mission and ethics, rather than just relying on the external evidence of a purported source within the Jesus tradition.[12] If we can establish a connection between mission and ethics in 2:12 on internal evidence within 1 Peter, Matthew 5:16 will provide important confirmation of a connection between mission and ethics and thus confirm our thesis that they are related in 2:12.

Along with the suggestion of a specific strand of the Jesus tradition as the background with which to understand this verse, there are three internal inferences that suggest understanding 2:12 as speaking of missional ethics. Firstly, I would like to suggest a parallel between 2:12 and 3:1–2. Both passages have *anastrophē* and *epopteuō* which are thematically linked, thus creating a linguistic connection. Furthermore, both passages focus on Christian relationships with outsiders in hostile contexts. It seems likely, therefore, that 3:2 be understood as a parallel instruction to 2:12.[13] If these statements are taken as parallel, it may help our understanding of 2:12.[14] Therefore, taking the phrase *ek tōn kalōn ergōn* as causal, along with *epopteuontes* as a causal participle ("because they see"), this suggests that the reason pagans will worship God on the day of visitation is because they have observed the beneficial deeds and conduct of these Christians.[15]

Secondly, we have in 2:12 a reference to the *present* conduct of these Christians and the *present* viewing of their conduct (cf. 3:2) as that which will cause them to glorify God on the day of visitation. It seems implausible to take the present verb, *epopteuō*, in 2:12 as a reference to a future viewing of their conduct on the day of judgment. It is, therefore, unlikely that this verse depicts the vindication of Christians at the eschaton, where their good works will be shown to be good by God.[16] Rather, we have good works being

---

12. For the argument see Best 1970: 95–113, here 109, who is generally skeptical of finding specific Jesus traditions in 1 Peter and states, "This is the clearest parallel in the whole of 1 Peter and is accepted as such by almost all commentators." Best 1970: 110 goes on to note that "it is highly probable that I Peter knew the tradition behind Matt. v. 16." See also Selwyn 1964: 171; Beare 1970: 111; Gundry 1967: 336–50, here 340.

13. Michaels 1988: 118 sees the situation as at least analogous. Seland 2009: 565–89, 577 states that 3:1 "is provided as an example of what 2:12 is all about." Elliott 2000: 468 states, "In 3:1–2 the same word [*epopteuō*] is used to express a virtually identical thought: honorable behavior, when observed, will win over nonbelievers."

14. Richard 2000: 128.

15. Seland 2009: 565–89, especially 575–79.

16. This is not to rob 1 Peter of the theme of the vindication of Christians, which is evident in 1 Peter 3:17–22; 4:17–19; 5:10.

portrayed as the means through which the gospel may be proclaimed in difficult circumstances. As in 3:1–2, the substance of Christian witness in hostile situations is also honorable conduct. By engaging in honorable conduct, they will hopefully persuade others to join them so that on the day of judgment, they too will glorify God.

Thirdly, that this refers not to the eschatological vindication of Christians,[17] but rather to pagans having joined the Christian community and thus praising God, is confirmed by 1 Pet 4:14 and 4:16 where it notes specifically that Christians glorify God. If only Christians glorify God, then the scenario assumes that at some point in the past these former pagans had converted, since they are now praising God.[18] The honorable conduct of the Christians will hopefully aid others in becoming Christians. "Despite the threat posed by the majority culture, the Christians must be actively involved in society and offer it witness. The substance of this witness is the good deeds of the Christians."[19]

We thus have three reasons from within 1 Peter to see 2:12 as pertaining to mission and ethics. It forms a parallel with 3:1–2, which is undoubtedly missional; *epopteuō* refers to the present viewing of beneficial works, not a viewing on judgment day; and in 1 Peter it is Christians, not pagans, who glorify God. If 2:12 reflects the Jesus tradition of Matthew 5:16, this offers further confirmation of a connection between mission and ethics.[20] Peter thus accommodates selected aspects of Graeco-Roman moral philosophy either shared by, or at least not contradicting, their Christian convictions as a means to help these Christians live honorable lives.[21] These activities are selected because they are deemed honorable by both God and pagans and thus allow these Christians to showcase the best of Graeco-Roman moral philosophy. This could occur in various contexts where Christians "honor everyone" (2:17), including the emperor and governing authorities (2:13–17), slaves obeying even harsh masters (2:18), and wives living with pagan husbands (3:1–6). This

---

17. Jobes 2005: 172.

18. Glorifying God is different from the eschatological recognition that Jesus is Lord portrayed in some early Christian texts such as Philippians 2:9–11.

19. Senior and Stuhlmueller 1983: 300.

20. Advocating ethical mission is a feature of several strands of early Christian teaching, e.g., Matt 5:14–16; Titus 2:10; Ignatius, *Eph.* 10.1–3. See especially Dickson 2003: 262–92; Trebilco 2007: 376–79.

21. Seland 2009: 588, "Words and works belong together as missional aspects of the lives of the Christians in the emergent church of 1 Peter."

honorable conduct would thus create a problem for hostile accusers because, on the one hand, they are maligning these Christians because of their conduct (2:12), but on the other hand, they are forced to reckon with their honorable deeds as well (2:12).[22] It is no wonder Peter expects hostile curiosity given the confusing impression early Christians must have created with their honorable conduct and yet utter disregard for other activities, including pagan idolatry (1:18; 4:3). By engaging in honorable conduct that benefits and blesses those who are hostile Peter hopes to correct the misunderstanding that Christians are public enemies.[23] Peter hopes the honorable conduct of believers would inspire questions and offer them an opportunity to defend the hope they have. There is, therefore, a definite relationship between mission and ethics, and Peter has accommodated various ethical ideas that cohere with the Christian vision of life in order that he may provoke Christians to honorable conduct, which will be a catalyst to conversion.

Negotiating Life with the World (2:13–17)

> **13** Because of the Lord, you should embrace your duty to every human creature, whether that is the emperor who is in charge **14** or of officials, commissioned by him to punish evildoers and to praise those who do what is beneficial. **15** It is God's desire that by practicing beneficial deeds you should mute the poor judgment of ignorant people. **16** So, as free people do not use your freedom as a pretext for evil but as slaves of God. **17** Honor everyone. Love the family of the faithful. Revere God. Honor the emperor.

The section of 2:13–17 offers specific instruction for Christians as they seek to navigate their lives amidst a culture which, both intentionally and unintentionally, sought to persuade them back to a former lifestyle. Here Peter gives instructions concerning civic authorities, pagan masters, husbands, and general interaction with unbelievers and how Christians should relate within these spheres of created structures that govern their lives. Peter

---

22. Schrage 1989: 279–81.
23. Cf. Tacitus, *Ann.* 15.44; Tertullian, *Apol.* 37.8; *Ad. Nat.* 1.7.8; Eusebius, *Hist. eccl.* 5.1.7.

begins this section in 2:13 with an imperative, *hypotagēte*. *Hypotassō* and cognates are used often in 1 Peter (2:13, 18; 3:1, 5, 22; 5:5).

Excursus: Fulfilling One's Duty as a Christian

According to Delling, the word *hypotassō* "embraces a whole series of meanings from subjection to authority on the one side to considerate submission to others on the other. As regards the detailed meaning, this can finally be decided only from the material context."[24] The term regularly functioned to describe a person placing themselves at the service of another or expressing duty or obligation to another.[25] The use of the middle voice in 2:18, 3:1, and 3:5 is indicative of a *voluntary* submission. Spicq states that "the use of the middle voice emphasizes the voluntary character of the submission and alleviates whatever might be humiliating about subordination, whatever suggests inferiority (Philo, *Decal.* 168; Josephus, *Ag. Ap.* 2.201)."[26] The nuances of this word can only be derived from the specific usage in context, but the notion of *authority* is not inherent in the word itself, as demonstrated by the usage in 2 Maccabees 13:23 and 1 Clement 38:1. In this context, the word has to do with finding a positive position in society, and not rebelling against "human creatures."[27] Achtemeier notes that it "advocates finding one's proper place and acting accordingly, rather than calling upon one to give unquestioning obedience to whatever anyone, including governing authorities, may command."[28] This finds further confirmation in the study of Richard, who suggests that *hypotassō*, has to do with one's *duty* toward others.[29] This is why we see the word "duty" or "obligation" as better describing the sense of *hypotassō* as used by Peter.[30] Kroeger confirms this by noting that Peter's intention is to advocate for a peaceful coexistence by fulfilling the duties of being a citizen within the given structures of society.[31]

---

24. Delling 1972: 8:45.

25. Luke 2:51; 1 Cor 14:32-40; 16:16; Eph 5:21; Titus 2:5.

26. Spicq 1994: 3:425n12.

27. Besançon-Spencer 2000: 110, "Submission is respectful cooperation with others."

28. See also Achtemeier 1996: 182; Richard 2000: 110-12.

29. Richard 2004: 412-20, here 417.

30. The language of "duty" is used by Thompson 1966: 66-78, here 69n36, 70, 72, 78; Barr 1961-62: 27-33, here 31.

31. Kroeger 2004: 82-88, here 83.

The author of 1 Peter sees these civic authorities as human creatures (2:13), deserving both duty (2:13) and honor (2:17).[32] Our author does not "demonize" these human agents, but encourages the audience to offer them the honor due to all of humanity (2:17). However, we should note that 1 Peter 5:8 may allow for a view that sees demonic influences operating behind and/or through various channels, leading to opposition to Christianity. To quell accusations of subversion or even sedition, Peter urges *duty* to governing authorities (2:13–14) and an intentional *honoring* of those in authority (2:17).

When the command to honor the emperor is made, it is made within the context of understanding that he is a human creature (2:13) and as such deserves honor. The author makes no differentiation or distinction between the type of honor (*timē*) due to the emperor and to other human creatures. This is suggestive of a limitation on the kind of honors that Christians may give the emperor. Thus, we see here a polite subversion of the veneration usually afforded to the emperor, which was common in Asia Minor at this time.

By aligning themselves with law-abiding and duty-fulfilling citizens and practicing what is beneficial, they will be able to mute the slander that is based on poor judgment and ignorance (2:15). By practicing a beneficial way of life, they will be able to neutralize the hostility that they are experiencing and hopefully find opportunities to respond to criticisms (3:15–16). Performing beneficial deeds serves both a pastoral strategy to alleviate suspicion and also to create missional opportunities. In view of ancient notions of reciprocity, Peter's expectation is that beneficial works would alleviate some of the social prejudice they were facing. As Bechtler notes, benefaction "is the only course of action God has willed the addressees to pursue in order to silence their accusers."[33]

This forms a connection to the next verse, which exhorts these Christians to paradoxically live as free slaves who belong to God. Peter provides another reason for their duty to those in official positions, namely their use of godly freedom. In the ancient world, "freedom" was a status one was born into or bought from one's owner. For Peter, it is due to our "new birth" that we are "free." Free from ignorance about God (1:14). Free from the

---

32. Williams and Horrell 2023: 1:730–31, rightly note the problems with taking *ktisis* as a reference to an "institution" rather than its usual referent to "creature" (cf. Tob 8:5, 13; Rom 8:39; Col 1:23; Heb 4:13).

33. Bechtler 1998: 162.

emptiness of our former lives (1:18). Free to embrace the new life that God has for us. In the ancient world, freedom did not entail unrestrained liberty to do whatever one wanted. That would be anarchy. For these Christians, their freedom is constrained and shaped by their allegiance to God. In early Christian literature, "slavery" is often used as a metaphor for total devotion to God.[34] Thus, they cannot use their freedom as a pretext (*echontes*) for doing evil or harm. Their primary allegiance is to God, which constrains and directs how they utilize their freedom. It also constrains and shapes how they honor the emperor and how they fulfill their duties as citizens, since God's will and ways are primary to all else.

The purpose of this pericope (2:13–17) is further to "warn the readers against assuming that as Christians they are free from normal political and moral restraints. Its point is to urge Christians to bring the same sort of responsible activity, characterized by love and humility, to secular contacts that they bring to their relationships within the Christian community."[35] Rather than develop hostile attitudes towards outsiders, these Christians are to appropriately honor the establishment and the people within it and not despise them (2:17; 3:11). They are to walk in the steps of Jesus, who offers a paradigm that is non-violent (2:21–25; cf. 3:9–12) in its attitudes and activities even towards those associated with the Roman Empire, which crucified Jesus. Peter's strategy here is help these Christians negotiate the hostile responses they are receiving as a result of their devotion to God. He does this by appealing to God's desire that they continue to exercise responsible duty to those in authority, practice beneficial deeds, do not abuse their freedom but understand their ultimate loyalty to God. By doing so, they will hopefully respond to mistaken assessments of themselves as dangerous or subversive people.[36]

The exhortation to "honor everyone" may appear innocuous to us, but it would have been explosive to first-century audiences. It was commonplace to consider honor to be due to those in power and authority, or to those through whom an advantage can be gained.[37] But here, Peter advocates "honor" to *all*, not just the elite, not just to those who can help them advance or do them favors. The Graeco-Roman world encouraged a careful and intentional calculation of who, when, and how worthy recipients

---

34. See Harris 1999.
35. Achtemeier 1996: 182.
36. See du Toit 2019: 237–39.
37. See du Toit 2023: 55–75, 68–69.

received honor. A fragment from Iamblichus states that, "People do not find it pleasant to give honor to someone else, for they suppose that they themselves are being deprived of something."[38] In contrast, Peter exhorts that honor is due to every single person they encounter. There is a beautiful (egalitarian?) vision here where all humanity is equal in status before God.

Two further instructions are found in 2:17, between the two exhortations to honor. The first is an imperative that these Christians should "Love the family of the faithful," referring to other Christians. Amidst the struggles of negotiating fidelity to God and the struggles to respond well to those in authority, and those hostile towards these Christians, Peter provides a pastoral instruction that they should love one another. They are family (*adelphotēs*), born of God, which means that they not only love God (1:8) but also each other (1:22; 4:8). This is followed by the instruction to "revere God." The emperor, along with every other human creature, deserves honor, but only God must be revered. The word for "revere" may in certain contexts indicate "fear" (3:6, 14) but when used of God indicates a profound reverence and awe (cf. 2:18; 3:2, 15).[39]

Negotiating Life as a Household-Slave (2:18–20)

> **18** Household-slaves, be dutiful to your masters with all deference, not only those who are kind and gentle but also those who are harsh. **19** For it is a credit to you if, being aware/conscious of God, you endure pain, suffering unjustly. **20** If you endure when you are beaten for doing wrong, what credit is that? But if you endure when doing what is beneficial and suffer for it, you have God's approval.

Slavery in the ancient world was a vile institution. That Seneca needed to argue that slaves could act virtuously and wisely (*Ep.* 47), and that Aristotle suggested that slaves could not attain virtue (*Pol.* 1.5.3–11), is indicative of the social situation faced by slaves in the ancient world. Aristotle's view was not uncommon as slaves were thought to be deficient in wisdom, virtue, and even humanity (e.g., Petronius, *Satira* 26).[40] This is illustrated by the idea that agricultural slaves are mere "speaking tools" (Varro, *On Agriculture* 1.17). Keith Hopkins states that slaves are to be seen as "distinct

---

38. Translation by Neyrey 1998: 18.
39. Achtemeier 1996: 188.
40. See Bradley 1994: 64.

from 'semi-articular tools' such as oxen, or 'dumb tools' such as carts. These definitions are yet further symptoms of the powerlessness and suffering of many slaves in Roman Italy."[41] Hopkins is careful to note that this was not the fate of all slaves in the first century and there were instances of slaves attaining status and honor, but these are exceptions to the general trend.[42]

However, before we address what the author is communicating, we need to note that Peter is not writing an essay on the legitimacy of slavery in the Graeco-Roman world. He is not writing to affirm or even regulate the subjugation and suffering of people. Rather, he is addressing the plight of Christians who find themselves in an impossible situation and how they can potentially navigate that situation while remaining faithful to Jesus. Slavery was a social institution that was part of the fabric of Graeco-Roman society, and Christians had to develop strategies to live within that terrible system, since they had little to no power to overcome it.

Peter writes to these Christians to practice their duty to their masters. That Peter addresses slaves of pagan masters seems probable for three reasons.[43] Firstly, Peter describes them as *skolios* (2:18). In this context, it is an adjective metaphorically describing someone whose character is "perverse,"[44] "unscrupulous,"[45] or "morally bankrupt."[46] This is consistent with the usage of the term in LXX Deuteronomy 32:5, Proverbs 16:28, Acts 2:40, and Philippians 2:15. Secondly, their actions are described as those who inflict *lypē* ("pain") and who act *adikōs* ("unjustly"). Finally, the masters are those who *kolaphizō*, "strike sharply" or "beat" (Matt 26:67; Mark 14:65) the Christian slaves (2:19).[47] This sets the context for Peter's instructions to Christian slaves with pagan masters. As property of pagan masters, it would have been difficult for them to separate themselves from them. Peter's instructions thus envision them remaining part of pagan households and specifically instructs them not to withdraw but to embrace their duties to their masters, whether those masters be cruel or kind. However, they are

41. Hopkins 1978: 123.

42. See Aristotle, *Oec.* 1.5–6; Xenophon, *Mem.* 2.1.16; Pliny the Elder, *Nat.* 33.6.26–27. Saller 1997: 133–53 outlines the violence often experienced by household slaves.

43. Christian masters in the early Christian tradition are instructed to treat slaves justly and reminded that God is their master and they will be judged for their actions. See Eph 6:9; Col 4:1; Did. 4.10; Ignatius, *Pol.* 4.3; Barn. 19.7.

44. Balz and Schneider 1990: 3:255.

45. BDAG 930.

46. Schreiner 2003: 137.

47. BDAG 555. See Tracy 2006: 279–96, here 288.

reminded of the priority of God and urged to continually be aware of God as they live their lives, always giving God ultimate allegiance, even if this incurs suffering.

The slaves addressed in 1 Peter are named *oiketai*, a common term describing household slaves.[48] As a subset of honoring those in authority (2:13, 17), Peter seeks in 2:18-20 to instruct household slaves to honor their masters by being dutiful to them, even under harsh circumstances.[49] Peter wants to instruct these slaves that they must not unnecessarily upset or rebel against masters, but rather seek to cope with the dreadful situation. In contrast to the common Graeco-Roman approach, which spoke to masters about slaves, we have the statements of 1 Peter that address the slaves themselves, thus giving them some honor, but more than this, they are said to have *syneidēsis* (2:19), which is a critical awareness, perhaps with a moral overtone in this context.[50] Thus Green helpfully writes, "Because in some circles in antiquity slaves were regarded as persons devoid of critical facilities, that Peter addresses slaves at all is significant; that he calls upon them to exercise discernment and moral agency in relation to the will of God is especially suggestive."[51] Furthermore, Peter's instructions to the slaves are qualified by the phrase *en panti phobō* (2:18), which most commentators rightly take as a reference to reverence for God.[52] Thus while Peter accommodates conventional instruction on the duty of slaves to masters, his instructions also subvert conventional ideas. Peter's manner of addressing slaves and the content of his message to them suggests a radically different portrayal of their honor and status within the Christian community. "The Petrine author, like other Christian writers, in no way shares the conventional notion that slaves are irrational brutes. He addresses them directly and not merely with a curt command but an extended line of argument assuming their rational competence, moral responsibility, and Christian commitment."[53] Peter therefore undermines conventional treatments of slaves by showing them respect through addressing them and attributing moral awareness to

---

48. BDAG 694. While the term is common in the LXX it is rare among early Christian writings (see Luke 16:13; Acts 10:7; Rom 14:4; 2 Clem. 6.1).

49. Holloway 2009: 183.

50. BDAG 967-68.

51. Green 2007b: 80.

52. Goppelt 1993: 193; Michaels 1988: 138.

53. Elliott 2000: 540.

them.⁵⁴ In 2:19, Peter acknowledges that slaves can be mistreated and suffer unjustly (*adikōs*). The Greco-Roman worldview denies any true injustice done to the slaves as slaves are property and non-human.⁵⁵ Peter dignifies these slaves, honoring them as those who rightfully deserve to be treated with virtue. They also have the ability to attain honor from God by doing the right thing (2:20). Furthermore, commentators regularly note that slaves play an exemplary role in 1 Peter.⁵⁶ These slaves are illustrative of the plight of other Anatolian Christians addressed by 1 Peter. Thus, we see no straightforward appropriation or repetition of the status quo, but rather a selective mode of thinking that both affirms and critiques ideas from the dominant culture. These ideas are shaped by specifically Christian values and convictions. The slaves addressed in 1 Peter provide an example of the kind of vulnerable negotiation that other Christians may have had to deal with in that context.

Peter's reference to the slave's duty is not a reference to *fear* or *reverence* of their masters, but rather reverence to God. Except for a quotation in 3:14, the usual referent for "fear/reverence" is towards God (cf. 1:17; 2:17; 3:2). Peter further notes that their duty is to be done "with a consciousness of God" (2:19). Then, they are reminded that doing good that incurs suffering receives "God's approval" (2:20). This provides not only the context for their obedience but also the priority of God over their masters in their decision-making and actions. Thus, as in verse 13, finding and occupying responsibly one's place in society, and not passive or unreflective subjection, is more to the point. As far as they are able, they are to perform their duties and serve their masters. There are limits to a Christian slave's obedience to human masters, since God is a higher master and thus allegiance to God takes precedence over human masters. This means, they will likely suffer for their primary allegiance to God. The question before them is whether they will suffer for the right reasons or the wrong reasons. If they suffer for the wrong reasons, that does not serve any purpose. However, if they suffer for their primary allegiance to God, and following his will and ways, there is at least some purpose to their suffering and they will gain approval, and vindication, from God.

54. Jobes 2005: 206.
55. Witherington 2008: 152.
56. On slaves and wives being exemplary models for the Christians addressed, see Achtemeier 1996: 192, 195, 209, 217; Boring 1999: 106–7; Green 2007b: 94; Bauman-Martin 2004: 253–79, here 255.

The Example of Jesus (2:21-25)

> 21 Because this is what you have been called to. The Messiah suffered for you, leaving you a paradigm in order that you would follow in his steps. 22 Jesus committed no sin, nor was any deceit in his mouth. Jesus was abused, yet he did not abuse them back. 23 When Jesus was suffering, he did not threaten in response. Rather, he entrusted himself to God, who judges righteously. 24 Jesus himself, carried our sins in his body to the cross. In order that, dying to sin, we may live for what is right. By his wounds you were healed. 25 Like sheep, you were wandering away, but now you have turned to the shepherd and guardian of your lives.

1 Peter 2:21–25 is the heart of this letter. It provides a vision of Jesus, shaped by the Scriptures, but adapted and applied to the specific situation faced by the Christians in ancient Anatolia. The negative and often painful implications of doing what is beneficial and right are noted here and repeated at 3:17; 4:15; and 5:10. Peter's purpose here is to exhort them to continue in this kind of embodied fidelity despite the often-negative consequences. However, we should clarify that suffering is not seen here as a virtue, but rather the probable result of doing God's will.

Jobes helpfully identifies the Isaianic references in this pericope.[57]

2:22 [He,] who did not commit sin, neither was deceit found in his mouth [Isa 53:9]

2:23 [He,] who when reviled *did not retaliate*, when he suffered, *he did not make threats* [Isa 53:7], but instead *trusted* [Isa 53:6, 12] *the one who judges justly* [Isa 53:8];

2:24 [He,] **who himself bore our sins** [Isa 53:4, 12] in his body upon the tree, so that being separated from sins we might live to righteousness;

[He,] by whose wounds you are healed [Isa 53:5].

2:25 For **you were like wandering sheep** [Isa 53:6], but now you have returned to the Shepherd and Overseer of your souls.

Peter's vision of Jesus is saturated in the Scriptures.

The conjunction *gar* and the pronoun *touto* in 2:21 refers back to 2:18–20 and, more specifically, to the issue of God's favor for slaves who

---

57. Jobes 2005: 194.

suffer for doing what is right and beneficial. Peter here responds that this is their calling, not to suffering but to live a life of holiness and blessing (3:9), which in that context inevitably led to suffering. The example of Jesus, who was innocent and yet still suffered, proves the point. But this was to be expected because Jesus had repeatedly predicted the suffering of his followers (e.g., Mark 8:34–38; 10:38–39; 14:27–28; Matt 10:25; Luke 21:12–16).

They have been "called" to live beneficial lives, lives that tangibly embody God's blessing and holiness, even if that leads to hostile responses and suffering. While the verb "called" may include their initial conversion (1:3), it refers to the vocation to be God's people who have not only been called "out of darkness and into God's marvelous light," but also to holiness (1:15) and ultimately into "eternal glory" (5:10).

That Christ "suffered for us," or "on our behalf," is not a reference to the benefits of the atonement (as it is in 3:18), but in this passage an indication that Jesus' sufferings are beneficial as an example of faithfulness to God despite the hostile response and physical violence that he endured. The following phrase makes that clear by appealing to Jesus as the quintessential paradigm of the Christian life. The ethical significance of Jesus' suffering on our behalf does not negate or devalue the soteriological significance, since they are two sides of the same work of Christ.[58] The word that I have translated here as "paradigm" (*hypogrammos*) was used by teachers in the ancient world to provide outlines to help children learn to write the alphabet.[59] It does not have to be an exact replica but rather a guiding vision, hence the word "paradigm." The circumstances of the Christians addressed by this teaching were different to those of Jesus, and yet Jesus is still the quintessential model for them to follow.

That this provides a model is clear from the quotation in verse 22 where Jesus' innocence is emphasized. Peter alters one word from the citation from Isaiah 53:9, where he uses the word "sin," rather than "lawlessness," probably to keep the example relevant to what has been said in 2:20 regarding slaves. Jesus did not commit sin (cf. 2 Cor 5:21; Heb 4:15; 7:26; 1 John 3:5). This makes his suffering even more shocking, but also relevant. Since these Christians are suffering for being Christians (cf. 4:16), they are mostly innocent of any real wrongdoing. The rhetorical function of this statement is thus to maintain their innocence with regards to wrongdoing. This would prove challenging with the next part of the verse, that no guile

58. Boring 1999: 122.
59. Schrenk 1964: 1:772.

was found in his mouth. The notion of "guile" has already appeared in 2:1 and will appear again in 3:10. Here it refers to any kind of manipulative invective. Verse 23 continues the theme of speech ethics. The author has composed this from various elements in Isaiah 53, in specific response to the contextual situation of these Christians.[60] First Peter 2:22b–23 then unpacks specifics of the example of Jesus that are relevant to his discourse and instruction. It is important to note that 2:21–23 goes beyond the passion and includes Jesus' life and ministry.[61] In this section, Peter focuses on the verbal aspects of Jesus' example. This is because the audience is facing predominantly verbal assaults (2:15; 3:9, 16; 4:14). Jesus maintained "a stance of nonretaliation in the face of precisely the kind of verbal abuse faced by the readers."[62] However, we should note that Jesus' sufferings ultimately led to the cross where he died, something our author and audience are aware of (2:24; 3:18). Just because Peter focuses on the verbal aspects does not exclude the physical maltreatment of either Jesus or the slaves who are likely being physically beaten.[63] A second feature of Jesus' response is his apparent silence (2:22–23). Jesus did not retaliate with abuse and threats, such as those that he endured. And for those called to emulate the paradigm of Jesus by walking in his footsteps, they are to refrain from verbal riposte and keep silent if necessary (cf. 3:1–2). Jesus offered himself in complete trust to God, who judges justly. Peter will later exhort Christians to follow this example, and entrust themselves to the faithful creator, while continuing to do what is right and beneficial (4:19), thus further confirming the exemplary nature of 2:22–23. God, who is both judge and creator, is faithful and can be trusted even in the most terrible of circumstances, perfectly illustrated by Jesus on the cross. He did not threaten, even though he could call down "more than twelve legions of angels" (cf. Matt 26:53).

With verse 24 we have a shift in focus from the exemplary to the soteriological. Not only is Jesus the model to emulate, but he is also the one who provides rescue and remedy for the malady of sin. The phrase "in his body" points to the vicarious nature in which he endured in himself the consequence of sins as "our" representative. Furthermore, some form of

---

60. See Jobes' references noted above.

61. Horrell 2014: 123–50.

62. Achtemeier 1996: 201.

63. If the slaves and wives are paradigmatic for what other Christians are experiencing, then it is possible that they too are facing physical suffering. However, 1 Peter's focus is social and verbal harassment.

substitutionary atonement is affirmed in this verse. Peter does not present the cross as an altar on which Jesus sacrifices himself. Rather, the image is closer to that of the purification offerings in Leviticus 4–6 and 16. Jesus, the pure and innocent one offers himself as atonement for us, those blemished and corrupted by sin. As Green helpfully notes, "For Leviticus sin pollutes, stains, and spoils, whereas sacrifice cleanses the effect of sin, cultic impurity. Sin has resulted in an estranged relationship between the sinner and God, and it is this separation that sacrifice addresses. 'Thus the priest shall make atonement on your behalf for the sin that you have committed, and you shall be forgiven' (Lev 4:35; see 4:31; 5:10, 13, 16, 18; 6:7)."[64]

The implications and purpose of such purification of sin are that they are now able to start "dying to sin,"[65] i.e., deal with it and begin to eliminate it from their lives (cf. 2:1; 4:3, 15). Sin is no longer their master, and they are free to live and do "what is right."[66] There is a necessary ethical component to the atonement (cf. 4:1–2). Jesus' death provides not only salvation but also an exemplar to model ourselves upon. Sin is decisively dealt with, which allows us to participate in Christ's life and embody Christ's example, i.e., righteousness or "what is right" (cf. 3:14), until we attain the full and eschatological salvation that Peter looks forward to (1:5).[67] Preachers may wish to explain this as the *problem* of sin, which is dealt with at the cross, the *power* of sin, which is dealt with in obedience to Jesus and the Spirit's power, and the *presence* of sin, which will be dealt with by God at the return of Jesus. Past, present, and future coalesce in Christ as the one who provides salvation to God's people. Or as Peter would say, "by his wounds we have been healed." The word "wound" is here a synecdoche representing his entire passion or suffering. The result for those who embrace the new life procured through Christ's suffering is that we are healed. Scholars disagree on what type of healing this refers to. Does this refer to physical healing or the spiritual healing of the effects of sin? Did this happen at conversion or is it an ongoing benefit throughout Christian life? Green offers a holistic view suggesting that "the two images—from death to life, and healing—speak to the same reality: cleansing for holiness."[68] This certainly began at the

---

64. Green 2007b: 89.
65. L-N 68.40; 74.27.
66. So Michaels 1988: 149.
67. There is some affinity here with Paul's teaching in Romans 6:11, 13, 18.
68. Green 2007b: 90.

point of conversion, but it must continue through our lives until we are completely sanctified in Christ eschatologically.

The change in topic from healing in verse 24 to wandering astray in verse 25 follows the text of Isaiah 53:5–6. The conjunction ("for") indicates an explanation for what precedes, and thus the healing referred to in verse 24 may point to conversion in verse 25. The same combination of *turning* and *healing* is found in Isaiah 6:10. Luke regularly uses *epistrephō* ("turn") as a term for conversion (Acts 3:19; 9:35; 11:21; 14:15; cf. 1 Thess 1:9). Because Peter identifies them as *sheep who were wandering astray*, we may be tempted to read this as speaking of the addressees belonging to the Christian community and then leaving, only to return at a later stage. However, that is not what Peter is intending here. He is describing their past conversion as seen from their current point of view. As pagans, they were wandering astray, living lives characterized by emptiness, futility, vice, and idolatry (cf. 1:18; 2:1; 4:3, 15). Then the transformative gospel of Christ came to them (1:23), through various evangelists (1:12), and offered them new life and hope in Christ (1:3). This new life is directed and protected by the Shepherd and Guardian, Jesus Christ. While Jesus the Chief Shepherd (cf. 5:4) is likely in view, this was a title reserved for Israel's God (Jer 23:3–6; 31:10; Ezek 34:11, 23–24; 37:24; Job 20:29). These former pagans are now God's flock (cf. 5:2), who are shepherded and guarded by Jesus. But recall at the beginning of the letter where we suggested that they are "protected by the power of God's faithfulness" (1:5). Thus, the roles and responsibilities of God and Jesus overlap. Once again, Peter pastorally attends to their troubled status as those who experience hostility and shame from outsiders, by reminding them of the pastoral care and concern of Jesus. This anticipates the discussion of leadership in 5:1–5 and the invitation in 5:7 to entrust themselves to God's care by throwing their anxieties and concerns at God.

Fusing the Horizon

To embrace the paradigm of Jesus faithfully today requires careful thinking and intentional embodiment that improvises the story of Jesus into our various contexts. As Jobes helpfully notes:

> Jesus Christ left us this pattern over which we are to trace out our lives, in order that we might follow in his footsteps. This is a strong image associating the Christian's life with the life of Christ. For one

cannot step into the footsteps of Jesus and head off in any other direction than the direction he took, and his footsteps lead to the cross, through the grave, and onward to glory.[69]

But what does this look like in our various contexts? Firstly, we must recognize and appreciate that the world is changing and God's people cannot remain static. As Vanhoozer notes: "The church is not called to play the same scene over and over but to take the gospel into new situations. To be faithful in its witness, the church must constantly be different. Indeed, at times we must even improvise."[70] The church is facing interesting times. Our responsibility is to embrace the promptings of the Spirit and the power of Scriptures in directing our christological paths and creatively engage a world that needs to know Jesus. Now, we should be careful to not insinuate that we are just trying to be different for the sake of being different. This misses the point, as Vanhoozer again notes, "Improvisation should not be equated with sheer novelty or with simply being original; on the contrary, improvisation depends on training, narrative skills, and a sense for what is appropriate to say and do in a given situation."[71] Improvisation requires skill (wisdom) and understanding (knowledge). We must understand how God's people have responded in the past, so that we can learn from both their victories and their failures.[72] Especially, and most importantly, we must faithfully and comprehensively understand Scripture and its story in which we find ourselves: for "it is precisely by gaining canonical competence that one is enabled to be creative and faithful in new contexts."[73] Thus, the more we understand the mission and message of God revealed in the Scriptures, the more we are able to appropriate God's vision for the future *into* the present. "Paradoxical though it may sound, memory is more important for improvisation than originality. The improviser is one who seeks not to create novelty but to respond to the past, for the future is formed *out of the past*."[74] The vision 1 Peter provides us with is a theological vision of what God has done and is doing (1:2), which provides us with new life (1:3), transformed by the gospel (1:23) so that we may live holy lives (1:15–16),

---

69. Jobes 2005: 195.
70. Vanhoozer 2005: 128.
71. Vanhoozer 2005: 128.
72. Dickson 2021 is a helpful example of this.
73. Vanhoozer 2005: 129. "Canonical competence" refers to a thorough understanding of Scripture. Scripture is the "canon," a word which means the "measuring stick." We use the canon (Scripture) to *assess* all our beliefs, values, performances, and structures.
74. Vanhoozer 2005: 339.

following the paradigm of Jesus (2:21) while we avoid vicious activities (2:1; 4:3, 15) and embrace a life of virtue (3:8) in Christian community (4:7–11). This provides a broad vision within which we may improvise our lives in ways that are appropriate and specific to our respective contexts.

Holy Living in the Home (3:1–7)

> ¹ Wives, similarly, be dutiful to your husbands, so that, even if some of them do not obey the message, they may be won without a word by their wives' lifestyle, ² when they see the integrity and reverence of your lives. ³ Do not fashion yourselves outwardly by plaiting your hair, and by wearing gold jewelry or designer clothing; ⁴ rather, let your inner self be adorned with the imperishable beauty of a gentle and peaceful attitude, which is priceless in God's sight. ⁵ This is how the holy women of times past, those who hoped in God, fashioned themselves by embracing duty to their husbands. ⁶ For example, Sarah obeyed Abraham and called him lord. You have become her daughters so long as you do what is beneficial and do not be intimidated. ⁷ Similarly, husbands fulfill your duty to your wives in your life together, demonstrating honor to the woman as the weaker vessel, since they too are heirs of the gracious gift of life—do this so that nothing may obstruct your prayers.

Missional Wives in Pagan Homes (3:1–2)

Peter begins by addressing another vulnerable group within the church, namely, Christian wives. The word "similarly" alludes back to the instructions given above at 2:13 concerning political leaders and 2:18 regarding slaves, and it is the same as the instructions given at 3:7 concerning husbands and 5:5 concerning members of the church. These wives are instructed to fulfill their duty to their husbands. Fulfilling their duty is not slavery to a dictator but a conscious decision. It is thus an exercise of the free. Peter is asking them to exercise their freedom well, "not as a pretext for evil" (2:16). However, careful attention to our text notes that there is a purpose clause ("so that") attached to the instruction of duty. The purpose clause can suggest that we are dealing here with "some" husbands who are not Christians, but others who are. Achtemeier rightly notes that "the interrogative particle *ei* states a fact here, not a hypothetical possibility."[75] Peter describes these husbands as those "who do not obey the message." "The message" here is a reference to the gospel.[76] Secondly, the tense of the word for "do not obey" is present tense, which indicates this is an ongoing rejection of the gospel, perhaps even a hostility to the gospel. Thus, we are dealing with a specific situation of Christian wives married to pagan husbands. These Christian wives are given an agenda, namely, to convert their pagan husbands. This is indicated by the word *kerdainō* ("to win over"), which was used by Christians as a missional term.[77] In 3:1, the author provides a strategy for mission once verbal proclamation has been decisively rejected. Rather than continue to proclaim the gospel, perhaps annoying or upsetting inter-personal relationships (and thus increasing their risk of abuse or violence), Peter's counsel suggests an alternative approach focused on their conduct, perhaps hoping that it will provoke questions that could be answered and a gospel that could be defended (3:15–16). But the focus here for Peter is on the ethical witness of these wives' lives. Just as in 2:12, it is the visible and patient practice of Christian virtue, directed towards God, which was to be their main strategy for Christian mission. Christians witnessed through their embodied character in the home, the marketplace, and public square as religious minorities who were consistently despised and yet were obviously a beneficial community that sought no harm to others. Purity and "reverence" are noted as causal factors in showing pagan husbands the way of truth found in the gospel. Purity would refer to both their sexual purity and their general holiness of character (1:15–16; 2:9–10). Reverence here is again reverence for God and indicates that God is the primary reference point for their lives. If these wives would embrace purity and reverence for God, pagan husbands might see the truth of who Jesus is in their lives and thus convert their allegiance to Jesus.

These qualifying comments indicate that the duty to pagan husbands instructed here is a qualified duty. Firstly, as in 2:13–17, "subordination to any human institution is conditioned by obedience to God."[78] Secondly, it was customary of pagan wives to worship only the gods of her husband.

---

75. Achtemeier 1996: 209.
76. See Pahl 2006: 211–27.
77. Cf. 1 Cor 9:19–22. See Daube 1947: 109–20.
78. Green 2007b: 91.

> A wife ought not to have friends of her own, but use her husband's as their common stock. And the first and most important of our friends are the Gods. A married woman should therefore worship and recognize the Gods whom her husband holds dear and these alone. The door must be closed to strange cults and foreign superstitions.[79]

But Peter is offering instruction here to Christian wives, which means their ultimate allegiance is to God, and they have forsaken the pagan gods of the household.[80] This was bound to cause friction in homes where the gods of the Graeco-Roman husband were to be exclusively worshipped.[81] When we combine this refusal to worship the household gods with the missional agenda advocated here, within the context of these Christian wives being exclusively devoted to God, we have ample reason to see why the duty instructed in 3:1 is not unilateral and unqualified but is rather subversive.

Fusing the Horizon

Integrity is a key to unlocking the power of the gospel. The *Oxford English Dictionary* defines integrity as: "Soundness of moral principle; the character of uncorrupted virtue, honesty, sincerity." For Peter, a Christ-like life is one of integrity, for the moral imagination is shaped by Christology, which informs a Christian's virtues and sincerity. Thus, a Christian understanding of integrity would be *the consistency of conviction embodied in character centered on Christ*. In today's "yeah, right!" society, where cynicism and skepticism are ubiquitous, integrity appears to be the only antidote to such vices, as a faithful presence disarms such toxic attitudes.

The importance of this is noted by Stackhouse, who devotes some space to the issue of integrity. He writes, "bad behaviour discredits the gospel, while good behaviour adorns and so commends it."[82] Stackhouse goes on to make the claim that "Augustine, for example, testifies that he was converted by the integrity and charity of other people, not merely by their Christian

---

79. Plutarch, *Advice on Marriage*, 19. See further Balch 1981: 84–86.
80. See du Toit 2021.
81. Balch 1981: 86 notes examples of this from early Christian history: *Recognitions of Clement* 2:29; Tertullian, *Apology* 3.
82. Stackhouse 2002: 135.

intelligence."[83] Hauerwas notes that our "preaching depends on the recovery of the integrity of the Christian community."[84] In our fractured and cynical environments, at stake is not always "what is true?" but rather, "who can be trusted?" This is illustrated by the German philosopher Nietzsche, who said, "I'm not upset because you lied to me, I'm upset because I don't trust you anymore."[85] This is illustrative of the results of a failure in integrity or a lack of integrity to begin with. Following Nietzsche's critique of metanarratives, and truth claims in general, he viewed these as nothing but "the will to power." The consequences are the same, a lack of trust in the person, and therefore especially the ideas, philosophy, or beliefs they are espousing. In such a climate, it is only through *faithful presence* of integrity that credibility can be restored.[86]

Integrity must provide the context in our various relationships through which we announce the gospel in words. Actions motivated not by self-interest but by a care, concern, and commitment to the well-being and benefit of others, prompted by the activity of God in our own hearts and communities, gives us integrity. However, this is not our aim. Our aim should be to please *God* and to live worthy of *him*. That is our focus. It just so happens that a by-product of such a focus and intention will give us the needed credibility to proclaim his message to others. As Guder notes, "it has to do with worthy living, with the character of our corporate life and the ways in which it provides evidence of the healing work of God's love, before a watching world."[87]

---

83. Stackhouse 2002: 135 then goes on to note 1 Peter 3:13–16 and quotes philosopher Linda Zagzebski as saying, "The experience of knowing holy people is still the most important evidence to me for the truth of Christianity."

84. Hauerwas and Willimon 1989: 164.

85. Nietzsche 2002: aphorism 183.

86. This seems to be part of the argument of Hunter 2010a, who uses the category of "faithful presence" as the focus of our missional endeavors. See Hunter 2010b, "Faithful presence is not about changing culture, let alone the world, but instead emphasizes cooperation between individuals and institutions in order to make disciples and serve the common good." Hunter 2010a: 234 further notes that "if there are benevolent consequences of our engagement with the world, it is precisely because it is not rooted in a desire to change the world for the better but rather because it is an expression of a desire to honor the creator of all goodness, beauty, and truth, a manifestation of our loving obedience to God, and a fulfilment of God's command to love our neighbor."

87. Guder 2003: 36–54, here 53.

Character and Conduct in the Household (3:3–4)

To appreciate the wisdom offered in 1 Peter 3:3–4, we must understand the negative attitudes, common in the ancient world, concerning the ostentatious dress of women. In his satirical critique, Juvenal describes how a woman keeps herself busy at home by "daubing her face, or listening to her lady-friends, or inspecting the widths of a gold-embroidered robe." Juvenal further notes,

> There is nothing that a woman will not permit herself to do, nothing that she deems shameful, when she encircles her neck with green emeralds, and fastens huge pearls to her elongated ears: there is nothing more intolerable than a wealthy woman. Meanwhile she ridiculously puffs out and disfigures her face with lumps of dough; she reeks of rich Poppaean unguents which stick to the lips of her unfortunate husband. Her lover she will meet with a clean washed skin; but when does she ever care to look nice at home? It is for her lovers that she provides the spikenard, for them she buys all the scents which the slender Indians bring to us. In good time she discloses her face; she removes the first layer of plaster, and begins to be recognisable.[88]

The issue here is the shame that such adornment incurs because it is the mark of a promiscuous woman who has neglected her household and her husband.[89] Thus Cohick perceptively notes, "Within the honor/shame culture that was the Mediterranean world at this time, a man's honor was most vulnerable at its weakest points—the women in his family and the friends he chose. A discussion about women is also a discussion about the men who are honored or shamed by the former's behavior."[90] Pagan thinkers suggested that dressing inappropriately is either immoral or shameful and thus brought dishonor and discord to the household and especially to the husband. This is the important cultural matrix within which to understand Peter's instructions in 3:3–4.

In verses 3–4, Peter outlines the areas in which duty is to be done to husbands: external and internal appearances. It is important for these women to understand that character is more important than clothing. This

---

88. Juvenal, *Sat.* 6.457–65 (LCL).

89. See further Aristotle, *Oec.* 3.1; Phintys, *Concerning the Temperance of a Woman* 153.15–28. On the braiding of hair, see Ovid, *Ars.* 3.136–38; Phintys the Neo-Pythagorean, *Concerning the Temperance of a Woman* 153.15–28.

90. Cohick 2009: 86.

injunction may sound peculiar to those reading it now. However, given the cultural context into which Peter writes, the instruction makes perfect sense. Women seen putting too much effort into their appearance were deemed morally suspect and having ulterior motives in seducing men. Jewish traditions also taught that excessive dress was sexually provocative and immodest (*T. Reu.* 5.1–5; Philo, *Virt.* 39–40; *Sacr.* 21) and could lead to the woman and her husband being dishonored for such extravagance. Davids notes, "Christian women are being exhorted to avoid appearing morally improper by the standards of their culture."[91] Again we see that Peter is encouraging a nonconformist attitude to the various cultural pressures faced by women, this time with regards to their fashion choices. As noted in 3:2, their conduct is to be shaped by purity and reverence. Their godly character is to shape their fashion choices, which reflect not only on them and who they are but also upon the rest of the household and Christian community. In contrast to the negative admonition of 3:3, in 3:4 Peter lauds the virtues of gentleness and peacefulness as what God deems truly valuable. Their character and conduct are to be focused on virtues, not vanities. It is important to note that the virtue of gentleness is not just for women (cf. 3:16) but also characteristic of Jesus (Matt 11:29).[92] Gentleness is contrasted with anger in Aristotle (*Eth. nic.* 4.5) and he states that a gentle person "tends not to look for revenge but rather to be sympathetic" (1126a3).[93] This is an important consideration for these wives as well as Anatolian Christians, as they negotiate the hostility of outsiders. Rather, they are to be those who are "peaceful," i.e., those who do not cause unnecessary disruptions and conflict (cf. 2 Thess 3:12; 1 Tim 2:2).

Holy Women in the Household (3:5–6)

These two verses provide the reason (*gar*) for the previous exhortation given in 3:3–4. The "holy women of times past" is probably a reference to standout characters such as Israel's matriarch's (e.g., Sarah, Rebekah, Rachel, and Leah). That Sarah is referenced in the next verse (3:6) makes this most likely. They are described as "holy women," which indicates their distinctive status as members of God's people and thus also their specific

---

91. Davids 2004: 224–38, 230.

92. Michaels 1988: 162 rightly notes that there is nothing distinctively feminine about these virtues since 1 Clement 13.4 and Barnabas 19.4 use them to describe all Christians.

93. Aristotle views gentleness as a deficiency, but the author of 1 Peter would disagree.

calling to live holy lives (cf. 1:15–16, referring to Lev 19:2; cf. 20:7, 26; 21:8). The opening "this is how" (*houtōs*) indicates that Israel's holy women fashioned themselves with a "gentle and peaceful attitude" (3:4). One of the ways this could be seen outworking in their lives was in how they fulfilled their duty to their own husbands.

While Peter uses the word "obey" *hypakouō* (3:6) to describe Sarah's relationship to Abraham, he cannot mean an unqualified obedience, as the situation is one where the wife cannot be completely obedient to her husband because, firstly, such ultimate obedience is reserved for Christ and secondly, she is trying to convert him.[94] The point of this passage, as with the comment on the slaves, is not to offer a timeless instruction but rather a highly specific strategy within a particular situation and context.

Peter also notes that Sarah called Abraham "lord" (*kyrios*), a title that could refer to one in charge of another, but was also a sign of respect in ancient Near Eastern culture.[95] The only time in Genesis that Sarah calls Abraham "lord" is found in 18:12, in a statement that does not indicate submission or obedience, but disbelief and perhaps cynicism.[96] Davids and Martin appeal to the *Testament of Abraham* as a possible background for understanding Peter's instructions concerning Sarah.[97] Davids notes that in this text Sarah often calls Abraham *kyrios*, "although only in casual or solemn discourse, not in contexts of 'obedience.'"[98] Martin also notes the idea of Sarah as the mother of the elect and the connection with good deeds.[99] The question becomes which background source is more appropriate for understanding Peter's instructions regarding Sarah. Since there is unlikely a literary connection between these two texts, this link seems questionable.[100] First Peter clearly has a connection to the LXX and Genesis in particular (3:20–21). Furthermore, *hypakouō* is connected to the Sarah

---

94. Even Grudem 1991: 194–208, 194–95 offers various qualifications on what "submissiveness" entails.

95. BDAG 577.

96. The appellation is common in Genesis (19:2; 23:6; 31:35; 33:8; 42:10). See Schelke 1988: 90n1 who refers to rabbinic texts that see Genesis 18:12–13 as a demonstration of Sarah's obedience. Examples include Gen. Rab. 47:1; 52:5.

97. See Martin 1999: 139–46.

98. Davids 2004: 232.

99. Martin 1999: 146.

100. Jobes 2005: 206. The date of the work and whether our author knew this work make the connection questionable. It may be that these ideas were perhaps common Jewish interpretive tradition.

and Abraham relationship, as well as Sarah's use of *kyrios* for Abraham. Thus, I am more inclined to see the Genesis narrative as the context within which to understand Peter's use of Sarah as an exemplar for these Christian communities.[101]

This leads us to the issue of obedience raised in 3:6 and how Genesis provides a context for such an instruction. There are various passages in Genesis that note Sarah's obedience to Abraham's request (Gen 12:13; 20:5, 13). However, we also have texts such as Genesis 16:2 and 21:10–12, which describe Abraham obeying Sarah. And the LXX uses *hypakouō* in Genesis 16:2 to describe Abraham's relationship to Sarah. This raises important questions about the background of Peter's instructions which we must address. In LXX Genesis 21:12, God said to Abraham, "whatever Sarah says to you, listen to her voice." There is mutual submission in the example of Abraham and Sarah that is directed at specific situations and contexts. This fits with what we have noted concerning Peter's strategy to convert pagan husbands to obey the word proclaimed by these wives. Sarah is not unilaterally obedient but has a voice in the Genesis narrative and is heard and obeyed. Her character thus exemplifies not only the virtues of obedience but also individuality and moral responsibility in making her own decisions and being heard.[102] This picture fits well with what we have described about the strategy of 1 Peter. There is a careful negotiation of when to obey and when to resist.[103] Although Sarah is not seen to be resisting in the Genesis narrative, she does make her own decisions and has a voice that is obeyed. The Genesis narratives depict Sarah taking responsibility and providing the means for Abraham to have an heir.[104] Sarah is exemplary

---

101. Kiley 1987: 689–92; Misset-van de Weg 2004: 50–62.

102. Michaels 1988: 166, points to the use of Sarah in the writings of Philo as one who embodies virtue. It remains speculative as to whether Peter and his audience were familiar with these discussions in Philo. Sly 1991: 126–29 suggests Philo and Josephus were embarrassed by some of the details concerning the Sarah and Abraham story and sought to depersonalize Sarah. However, it is unclear whether Philo's personification of Sarah as virtue is intended as a negative.

103. Misset-Van De Weg 2004: 53 suggests that the model of the matriarchs (Sarah, Rebecca, Rachel, and Leah) can be characterized as those who *complied* and *rebelled*.

104. Misset-Van De Weg 2004: 57 reviews the evidence from the Genesis narrative concerning Abraham and Sarah and concludes: "From the Abraham-Sarah cycle a picture emerges of a beautiful and strong woman who is of great value to her husband. He prospers because of her, and she bears him the son of the promise. She is a woman who takes initiatives and fights for that to which she thinks she and her son are entitled and finds God on her side, who tells her husband to listen to her."

in her initiative and her responsibility, as well as her selective obedience, and it appears from 1 Peter that this is precisely the role model needed for these women. Westfall is right to note that "Peter equips vulnerable women to behave differentially with courage, that is, without being motivated by intimidation or worry."[105] The statement "You have become her daughters" speaks to the incorporation of these former pagan women into the people of God. As such, Sarah provides a role model for these Christian women who are called to be morally aware and responsible agents who seek to live virtuous lives in the hopes of converting their husbands to Christ. They are not to be "intimidated" or "terrified" by their pagan husbands, nor are they to rebel or become unwisely disobedient. Rather, they are called to careful negotiation whereby they virtuously fulfill their duties, but nonetheless resist certain elements of conformity to Graeco-Roman standards of praxis regarding women. The particularities of the situation with these women must be kept at the forefront of our attention lest we too quickly try and move to the contemporary significance of such an instruction.

Holy Men in the Household (3:7)

This verse forms almost an afterthought to the main consideration of the precarious situation of these wives. While translations consistently offer "husbands" as the translation of *hoi ándres* (e.g., NRSV; CEB; NKJV; NIV), Achtemeier suggests that the use with *gynaikeios* suggests that we understand the former as men in the household in contrast to the female members of the household.[106] What Peter is addressing in this verse is "the way males in a household deal with its female members."[107] This is certainly a possible reading. While I think it likely that the *hoi ándres* refers to husbands, the use of *gynaikeios* could certainly broaden the instruction to include all men of the household.

The sentence lacks a verb, which points back to the previous times the "in the same way" construction has been used (3:1; 5:5). In the same way as what? First, Dubis rightly notes that there is a difference between the way slaves will fulfill their responsibilities to their masters and the way wives or husbands fulfill their responsibilities to one another.[108] Secondly,

---

105. Westfall 2011: 243.
106. Achtemeier 1996: 217.
107. Achtemeier 1996: 217.
108. See Dubis 2010: 84.

we must ask, to what does *homoiōs* refer? Achtemeier suggests that it refers back to the imperative in 2:17.[109] This seems unlikely as all the groups specifically addressed have been reminded of their *duty* (2:13, 18; 3:1; 5:5). Furthermore, the use of "similarly" specifically refers to "duty" in 3:1 and 5:5, suggesting that the implied verb be taken as "be dutiful to," in which case this verse outlines the specific duty of Christian husbands to Christian wives.[110] The reason we understand this as referring to Christian wives is because Peter describes them as "co-heirs of the grace of life," indicating they are among God's people.

Senior suggests that the phrase "according to knowledge" is better understood as "'with awareness' *(kata gnōsin)*, that is, with the kind of 'consciousness of God' (2:19) or 'reverential fear of God' (3:2) that was also enjoined on the slaves and wives."[111] These husbands must have knowledge of how best to live with their wives, not arbitrarily following or adopting the cultural norms but instead living holy lives together with their wives in an honorable manner. This is because the women are described as "weaker" *(asthenēs)*.

Since "weaker" provides a comparison with other vessels, both men and women are understood as "vessels," with women being the "weaker" kind. Elliott wants to limit this to a physiological weakness. "'Weaker' represents nothing more than the universally held notion that females, and thus also wives, are biologically weaker and more vulnerable than their male counterparts and thus require the particular consideration of the latter."[112] While this is certainly part of the issue, we must acknowledge that in the Graeco-Roman world, women too often experienced social weakness, being perceived as inferior, neglected, insulted, ignored, or disparaged in some way. Thus, we should not delineate the boundaries of "weakness" too much. As Davids notes, "The point is that the husband is in some respect "stronger" and needs to recognize this fact in his life with his wife, so that he does not exploit this disparity in strength, consciously or unconsciously."[113]

In a cultural context where women were in weaker social positions, these Christian husbands are instructed to "assign" or "demonstrate" honor,

---

109. Achtemeier 1996: 209.

110. So also Davids 2004: 237.

111. Senior and Harrington 2003: 83.

112. Elliott 2000: 577–78. See also Achtemeier 1996: 217; Cranfield 1954: 91; Goppelt 1993: 222.

113. Davids 2004: 237.

and thus provide social status to them. Honor is not to be thought of as some internal appreciation or respect. Rather, honor is embodied in treating them virtuously through either verbal or physical acts that give them social standing.[114] Peter provides two theological reasons for why they should be treated with honor. Firstly, they are "co-heirs of the gift of life," and as such there is an equal standing between them and other members of the people of God. This entails treating women with all the virtues mentioned in this letter (e.g., 3:8) and avoiding all the vices with regards to them (2:1; 4:15). Secondly, a failure to honor one's wife, and other women within the household, has serious consequences with regards to one's relationship with God. Peter indicates that a failure to treat women with honor as equal heirs will entail an obstruction to their relationship with God. As Achtemeier forcefully notes, "The point is clear: men who transfer cultural notions about the superiority of men over women into the Christian community lose their ability to communicate with God."[115] This is a somber reminder of the implications of those with social power to use their abilities in a manner that expresses their virtuous duty to others, particularly those who are socially weaker. There is a necessary correlation between one's ethics and one's prayer life. Honor to others inclines the ear of the Lord.

Characteristics of Holy Living (3:8–12)

> 8 Finally, all of you, have concord, sympathy, love for each other, a tender heart, and a humble disposition. 9 Do not return evil for evil or insult for insult, but return such with a blessing. This is your calling—so that you may inherit a blessing. 10 For "Whoever wants to love life and to see good days, let them keep their tongues from evil and their lips from speaking deceit. 11 Such people must turn away from evil and do good; seek out peace and go after it. 12 Because the eyes of the Lord are upon the just, and his ears attentive to their prayer. The face of the Lord, however, is against those who perform evil deeds."

What kind of community must the church be to engage faithfully with a world that is mostly set against it? Here the author outlines key virtues that these Christians should embody that will aid them in this endeavor. It is only as the community practices such virtues that they will then be able

---

114. du Toit 2023: 65–68.
115. Achtemeier 1996: 218.

to practice the way of Christ instructed for them in 3:9, in which they are urged to forsake the way of retaliation and instead offer blessings to those who verbally, or even physically, assault the Christian community.

In verse 8 the author offers five virtues that are to characterize these Christians and their relationships among one another. The virtue of having "concord" (*homophrōn*) or being "like-minded"[116] indicates that they have similar beliefs, values, and commitments (cf. Phil 2:2). It is possible that this virtue is the overarching characteristic into which the other four fall and provide examples of what it means to have the same pattern of thought. Sympathy (*sympathēs*) is also instructed, and the difficult situations these Christians are currently facing makes this a pastorally important virtue for everyone in the community to practice. The author of Hebrews notes, "you had sympathy for those who were in prison" (Heb 10:34). The writer of Hebrews furthermore uses the word of Jesus in his solidarity with the Christian community. "For we do not have a high priest who is unable to sympathize with our weaknesses, but we have one who in every respect has been tested as we are, yet without sin" (4:15 NRSV). Embodying sympathy at the plight of sisters and brothers facing "fiery trials" should inspire one to acts of love for the family. This sympathy is specifically directed at the Christian community as the family of Christians, but the rest of 1 Peter makes clear that such love will overflow to others as believers do what is beneficial, particularly for outsiders (2:12, etc.). It is not clear what the difference is between the "sympathy" already mentioned and "tender-heart" used here. Selwyn suggests *eusplanchnoi* refers to "courage," but the use in Ephesians 4:32 speaks more to a "tender-heartedness" or a pastoral sensitivity. Such a pastoral sensitivity would make better sense with the context of Christians suffering. Finally, the addressees are instructed to practice humbleness, which was not considered a virtue in the Graeco-Roman world.[117] A helpful unpacking of this concept is found in Romans 12:16, "Live in harmony with each other. Don't be too proud to enjoy the company of ordinary people. And don't think you know it all!" (NLT).

Moving from insider-related virtues, which may spill over into communal relationships, Peter now offers explicit instruction (3:9) regarding how to engage with people hostile towards them. In the Roman world, revenge was an integral social obligation to maintain one's honor in society. According to Cicero, "Nature has two parts: giving everyone what is

---

116. L-N 30.21.
117. du Toit 2022: 87.

his due and the right of revenge" (*Topica* 90).[118] Following the teaching of Jesus, Peter shockingly exhorts these Christians to not enter the cycle of harm and destruction that reciprocity entails. Both the teachings of Jesus (Matt 5:38–44; Luke 6:27–28) and his praxis (1 Pet 2:22–23) are to be determinative for these Christians. This tradition is also taken up in Pauline literature (Rom 12:17; 1 Cor 4:12; 1 Thess 5:15; cf. Rom 12:14; Eph 4:1–3; Col 3:13). While facing insults and abuse, they should not return like for like, even though that is what is culturally expected of them. Rather, they should break the cycle of abuse and violence and respond positively with a blessing (Mark 10:16; Luke 24:50).

Here in 3:9, following the christological paradigm of 2:23, the Christians are again instructed to avoid the riposte of verbal assaults and evil activity. Peter uses the substantive, *loidoria* (cf. the verbal form in 2:23), here, which indicates "speech that is highly insulting."[119] The use of the same word in 3:9 connects these two passages and shows that Peter is appealing to the example of Jesus, not just as appropriate to household slaves, but to all Christians seeking to be faithful in how they respond to such slander.

Not only are they to refrain from sparring with others but in response to their slurs and evil deeds, they are to reciprocate with a *blessing* (*eulogeō*).[120] It is possible to limit the sense of *eulogeō* to saying "something commendatory,"[121] or merely "speaking well of," those who slur these Christians. "By such a tactic one ignores the insult as a challenge, thereby extricating oneself from the socially destructive cycle of challenge-retaliation, and shifts the subject from shame to honor, from defamation to praise."[122] This would follow the instruction of 2:17, "honor everyone" (*pantas timēsate* cf. Diogn. 5.15).

However, scholars have suggested a wider reference to the concept of *blessing*, including prayer (cf. Matt 5:44; Luke 6:28; Did. 1:3).[123] "The response of believers to hostile words goes beyond answering insult with praise and actually involves 'prayer for those who abuse' (Luke 6:28) that

---

118. Blundell 1989: 26 notes that "Greek popular thought is pervaded by the assumption that one should help one's friends and harm one's enemies."

119. BDAG 602.

120. Schelke 1988: 94n2 sees a connection with 2:5, 9 and the priestly call of these Christians.

121. BDAG 408.

122. Elliott 2000: 608.

123. Michaels 1988: 178.

God might endow them with the benefits of salvation."[124] Given that they are to "inherit a blessing," which seems more likely to refer to the benefits of their salvation (1:4), the reference to blessing here may be wider than just responding with kind words.[125] This idea is strengthened when we consider the Hebrew Scriptures and their understanding of blessing as a tangible benefit or gift.[126] "The purpose of the gift can be to express thanks, to express friendship, or to appease an angry person. The desired perlocutionary effect is to make the recipient favorably disposed toward the donor."[127] This is illustrated in Genesis 33:11 and 1 Samuel 25:27, where the blessing or gift is intended to appease an irate foe.[128] Thus, Peter's instructions are to go against the convention of revenge and to respond with kindness and a tangible benefit as the means of breaking the cycle of hostility and appeasing outsiders.

This is their "calling," a notion that appears in 1 Peter at critical moments (cf. 2:9, 21; 5:10). One cannot help but hear an echo of the calling of Abraham in Genesis 12:1–3, where he and his family were blessed in order to be a blessing. The notion of "calling" could therefore be vocational in the sense that this is what God's people have always been called to, and this continues with these Christians. They have been "called" to be a presence in the world that embodies and confers the blessings of God in tangibly beneficial ways.

The quotation from LXX Psalm 33:13–17 establishes Peter's point by providing a scriptural rationale for the instruction given in 3:9. Rather than participate in the verbal riposte, if they want to live flourishing lives as God intended, they will avoid allowing their speech to get the better of them (v. 10). This involves two components (v. 11). Firstly, they are to deviate away from any harmful or negative practices. Secondly, they are to practice what is beneficial for others. The goal of such rejection and pursuit is peace, which is not to be defined merely as the absence of anxiety or strife but rather flourishing in all its dimensions. We must remember that this is an instruction set within the context of engagement with hostile outsiders, and so while they may be tempted and even culturally encouraged to respond

---

124. Green 2007b: 106.
125. Elliott 2000: 608.
126. See Mitchell 1987: 79–131.
127. Mitchell 1987: 126.
128. This strategy of making friends of enemies is also present in the Graeco-Roman world, see du Toit 2019.

negatively, here Peter instructs to forsake the path of revenge and instead to pursue the path of peacemaking. Such an instruction is given further theological justification from the psalm (v. 12). Not only is God attentive to and aware of the righteous (i.e., those whose lives are characterized by holiness and the example provided by Jesus), but God is also against those who do what is harmful and destructive (i.e., the opposite of holiness and the paradigm of Jesus). The way these Christians live shapes their relationship to God. Peter has already noted that a failure to honor women in the household will negatively affect their relationship with God. Here again, a life that embraces evil, deceit, and unrighteousness will make an enemy of God.

Fusing the Horizon

"Sticks and stones may break my bones, but words will never harm me." This may be one of the biggest lies ever told. Because according to Proverbs, *the tongue* carries the power of life and death (Prov 18:21). Strange to think that we could kill the life of a human being, just with our words. Sure, they may not be physically dead, but psychologically and socially, their "lives" could be destroyed by the words that are spoken. Psychologists, counsellors, and social workers are quick to realize the incredible power words have on personalities, social integration, and community harmony. In fact, you could easily close your eyes right now and imagine various conversations that have cut you. I have a vivid memory of my principal in high-school articulating in no uncertain terms that I was a complete waste of oxygen, and I would never amount to anything significant. At the time those words were uttered, I had no idea the impact would linger for years to come. In my mind and in my actions, retaliation was easy and achievable. But Peter offers these Christians a path out of the sick-cycle-carousel of verbal insults, abuse, and violence. For those who want to flourish, to live life as God intended it, we must take care with our words.

> Our communities should offer the world the gift of a community that speaks gently both to its members and to outsiders, a community that knows how to speak both rightly and kindly. Only communities who have learned to speak like this can make peace after conflicts have escalated emotions, and vicious and aggressive language has compounded harm with harm, whether these disputes take place in

the office, at the local café, after a church meeting, over international borders, or over the kitchen table. Where violent speech deepens a dispute, gentle speech can begin to defuse it. Such speaking flows from peace and fosters peace.[129]

It seems that at this time in our fragile world, the wisdom of how, when, and whether to speak is one that is vital to the healing and flourishing of relationships between Christians and those not-yet a part of the family. It is also imperative that those within the Christian community embrace the same ethic advocated here. We should aim for concord, sympathy, and love for each other in the words we speak to one another. A tender heart and a humble disposition would do much to facilitate the healing of past hurts, misunderstandings, and mistakes as well as to foster trust as we seek to navigate and negotiate what the future might look like.

---

129. Campbell 2020: 348.

Exhortations to Communal Flourishing Amidst Opposition (3:13—5:11)

A Holy Life Amidst Suffering (3:13-17)

> 13 Who will mistreat you if you become zealous for what is good? 14 But if you do suffer for doing what is right, you are blessed. Do not be afraid of them or troubled by them, 15 instead sanctify the Messiah as Lord in your hearts. Always be prepared to answer everyone who asks you about the hope that is among you; 16 but do this with gentleness and reverence. Maintain a good conscience, so that, when you are slandered, those who mistreat you will be put to shame because of your beneficial conduct in Christ. 17 It is better to suffer doing what is good, if that is God's will, than to suffer for doing evil deeds.

Having concluded the previous section with an instruction to avoid retaliation, seek peace, turn from evil, and do good (3:9–12), the author now wrestles with the consequences of these actions. The section begins in 3:13 with a rhetorical question about doing good and ends in 3:17 with the instruction that if faced with a choice, suffering for doing good is better than suffering for doing evil (3:17). Peter instructs them to be "zealous" for what is beneficial or good. While the focus in this pericope is clearly on suffering, 3:15–16 provide a brief tangent on the possible response that may occur: curiosity. In response to the hostile curiosity they face, Christians are instructed to offer a response that is shaped by virtue.

While one might expect doing what is beneficial to others to neutralize the insults and abuse of these Christians, that is not always the case.[1] Peter thus seeks to pastorally prepare them for further negative responses and how to handle them. Rather than view this suffering as shameful, Peter reframes it as a blessing (3:14). When such suffering occurs, they are to realize that they are blessed (by God) who will provide them ultimate protection (1:5). Rather than be afraid or troubled, they should respond appropriately. With Christ as Lord of their lives (3:15), Peter instructs them to "always be prepared," not knowing when they will be challenged. However, when challenged they are to offer a reasoned response. While the context of this response may include legal contexts (Luke 12:11–12; Acts 22:1; 25:16; 2 Tim 4:16), it may also include private disputes (1 Cor 9:3; 2 Cor 7:11), and that is more likely the case here. This refers not to an individual hope within the Christian, but rather the "hope that is among you" as Christians.[2] "Hope" is in the future act of God's salvation, which shapes the posture of Christian life (1 Pet 1:3, 13, 21; 3:5). It is thus reminiscent of the way Paul sometimes uses the word *pistis* (e.g., Rom 14:22; 1 Cor 16:13). Peter instructs these Christians to react to hostile curiosity with a defense or explanation of the Christian hope shaped by the virtues of *prautēs* and *phobos*. *Prautēs* is a common Christian virtue found in the virtue lists of Galatians 5:23, Ephesians 4:2, and Colossians 3:12, but its semantic range is wide. It is translated as "gentleness" (NIV, NRSV) and "meekness" (KJV). In contrast to being abrasive or callous, it refers to an attitude that is tender. It thus likely reflects *praus* in 3:4 and is also conceptually related to *tapeinophrosynē* (5:5, 6). Jobes states that here *phobos* "refers to an attitude toward others that is rooted in one's attitude toward God."[3] This seems the best way to take the reference to *phobos*, which usually indicates reverence towards God (1 Pet 1:17; 2:17, 18; 3:2).[4]

> The exhortation is especially pertinent because in an honor-and-shame culture, the natural response of anyone offering a defense would be to do so at all costs, including slander. Christ has already been given as an example of not returning verbal abuse (2:23), with Ps 34 further supporting this posture (3:10–12).[5]

---

1. See du Toit 2019.
2. Jobes 2005: 230; Achtemeier 1996: 233.
3. Jobes 2005: 231.
4. Michaels 1988: 189.
5. Watson and Callan 2012: 86.

The virtues of *gentleness* and *reverence* must shape the Christian's response to hostile curiosity. But importantly for us here is the connection between *agathos/agathopoieō* (used four times in 3:13–17) and mission. The consistent reference to *agathos*, which is equated with *dikaiosynē* in 3:14 and *anastrophē* in 3:16, makes it clear that it is Christian praxis that is the cause of hostility and curiosity. Christians are to respond to hostile curiosity in a manner that explains and defends the hope they profess and the praxis they embody.[6] Their words are to interpret their actions. We thus see an analogous situation to that of 3:1–2 where wives are instructed to conduct themselves honorably towards those who have rejected the gospel, with the hope that their lives will validate their message and ultimately convert their husbands.

> They need to rely on dialogue and exchange. Christians are supposed to give a personal answer to those who ask them the reasons for their hope (3.15–16). This answer, based on dialogue, is accompanied by people being able to witness by their good deeds, and is clearly a missionary tool for a community that does not turn its back on the world around it.[7]

Most importantly for our purpose is to note that this response to hostile curiosity is set within the context of a discussion concerning their praxis, which includes: *agathopoieō* (3:13–17), *dikaiosynē* (3:14; cf. 3:12), and *anastrophē* (3:16). As noted below, there is much discussion regarding what *agathopoieō* includes, but at the very least it includes honorable deeds that benefit or bless others. In 3:9–12, the Christians are instructed to break free from the cycle of reciprocating evil and abuse and instead to repay hostility with acts of blessing. They are specifically instructed, *poiēsatō agathon* (3:11), namely, to *do what is beneficial*. Therefore, the instruction to respond to hostile curiosity in 3:15–16 is based on the honorable conduct of these Christians providing the reason for pagan curiosity. "Peter sees his readers as being 'on trial' every day as they live for Christ in a pagan society."[8] This honorable conduct includes the best of Graeco-Roman moral philosophy that overlaps with various Christian convictions and would include the shared ethical instructions discussed in our chapter on

---

6. Achtemeier 1996: 234, "Cultural isolation is not to be the route taken by the Christian community. It is to live its life openly in the midst of the unbelieving world, and just as openly to be prepared to explain the reasons for it."

7. Tàrrech 2008: 242.

8. Michaels 1988: 188.

acculturation (2:1; 2:13—3:7; 3:8; 4:15). Peter concludes this section in verse 17 with a comment that can be misunderstood. Peter notes that it is better to suffer as those who are living a beneficial life than to suffer for doing what is wrong or evil. In the middle of this statement, however, is a comment regarding God's will. Peter is not suggesting that God wills their suffering, but rather that God wills their living a beneficial life. The kind of life that God wills can result in suffering (2:12; 4:4). The idea is similar to that found in Matthew 5:10, where opposition is expected for living a life shaped by what is right, which for Peter is determined by the character of God (1:15-16) and the conduct of Christ (2:21). They should not suffer for doing evil (cf. 2:20) but rather be prepared to suffer for doing what is right. God will ultimately vindicate those who do what is right and punish those who do evil (3:10–12).

Excursus: Beneficial Deeds in 1 Peter

The theme of "good works"—or as I have translated it, "beneficial deeds"—is an important and central theme in 1 Peter (2:12, 14–15, 20; 3:6, 11, 16–17; 4:19).[9] We also have references to "honorable deeds" (2:12), "beneficial conduct" (3:16), doing what is beneficial (3:11), and the rhetorical invitation to be "zealous for what is beneficial" (3:13). I have elsewhere argued that the purpose of 1 Peter's focus on beneficial deeds is twofold. Firstly, it provides an ethical witness for these Christians (2:12; 3:1–2).[10] Secondly, it is hoped by the author that such beneficial deeds will reduce the social harassment from outsiders (2:14–15; 3:13).[11] However, the author is realistic in his hopes and understands that despite their beneficial deeds, they may still experience social harassment or harm (2:20; 3:14; 4:19). This is because they belong to Christ as Christians (4:16) and refuse to participate in pagan idolatry (4:3).[12]

The question scholars have grappled with is what constitutes "beneficial deeds." Bruce Winter has argued that "doing good" in 2:14 refers to public benefaction and civic responsibility.[13] This could include supplying food during times of famine, "refurbishing the theatre, widening roads, helping in the

---

9. See the excursus of Williams and Horrell 2023: 1:712–18.
10. du Toit 2019: 241–42; Volf 1994: 25; Elliott 2000: 495.
11. du Toit 2019: 226–32.
12. See du Toit 2021.
13. Winter 1988: 87–92.

construction of public utilities," and "helping the city in times of civil upheaval." However, it is unlikely that the Christians addressed in this letter have the economic means to practice such benefaction.[14] Williams and Horrell prefer to understand Peter's use of the concept of good works as "designed for the benefit of insiders, not outsiders."[15] They write, "By appropriating the language of wealth and privilege and then reinscribing it with a new (Christianised) meaning, the Petrine author seeks to reshape the social identity of a group that has been marginalised by society. Since the redefinition of good works was in accordance with a standard in which the audience could excel, they would be able to achieve a much more positive outcome and, consequently, a positive self-concept."[16] While there is clearly a concern for encouraging a positive self-concept among the Christians addressed by this epistle, I am not persuaded that this is the purpose of Peter's use of the theme of good works. Firstly, if we look at where the concept is used, it is primarily in contexts where Christians interact with outsiders (2:12; 2:12, 14–15, 20; 3:11, 16–17; 4:19), and not with reference to their self-concept. Secondly, there is significant discussion of how to alleviate social hostility in the ancient world. I have explored this theme in more detail elsewhere, but here cite one example:

> In *Aesop's Fables* we are told that "Many people will not hesitate to confer a benefit on their enemies for the sake of gain" (*Fab.* 3). The philosopher Diogenes Laertius (third century CE) states "It is right to confer benefits (*euergetein*) on a friend in order to bind him closer to us, and on an enemy in order to make a friend of him" (*Vit. Phil.* 1.91). These statements illustrate a strategy for dealing with hostility and conflict in the ancient world.[17]

It is my view that this is precisely what the author of 1 Peter hopes to achieve, the winning over of those who are hostile through the practice of beneficial deeds. Set within the context of reciprocity and gratitude in the ancient world, those who experience benefits from these Christians may realize that they are not "haters of humanity" (Tacitus) but rather those who are called to bless outsiders and seek peace with them (1 Pet 3:9–10). Furthermore, the concept of beneficial deeds and honorable conduct is utilized in missional contexts (2:12; 3:1–2, 9–12, 15–16). The burden of our author is to help Christians

---

14. See the critique of Williams 2014: 68–104.
15. Williams and Horrell 2023: 1:718.
16. Williams and Horrell 2023: 1:718.
17. du Toit 2019: 226.

navigate and negotiate life amidst hostility, seeking to help them remain faithful to Jesus but also to the mission of Jesus to recruit others for salvation.

The Example of Jesus (3:18-22)

> 18 This is because the Messiah also suffered for sins once for all, the just one for the unjust ones, in order to lead you to God. He was put to death by the flesh, but made alive by the Spirit, 19 in which he ascended and made an announcement to the spirits in prison. 20 These disobeyed long ago, when God waited with patience in the days of Noah, during the construction of the ark. Only a few, that is, eight lives, were saved through water. 21 The corresponding item, baptism, now saves you—not as a removal of dirt from the body, but as a commitment of a good conscience to God, through the resurrection of Jesus the Messiah, 22 who has ascended into heaven and is at God's right hand, with angels, authorities, and powers obligated to him.

Martin Luther said: "This is as strange a text and as dark a saying as any in the New Testament, so that I am not yet sure what St. Peter intended."[18] The complexity of the issues should encourage humility in our interpretations. The varied history of interpretation of this passage should also discourage overconfidence in our interpretations.[19] For example, some early church fathers taught that this passage referred to the *descensus*, the descending of Christ into hades to proclaim redemption to the saints of the old covenant.[20] Others taught that this passage referred to the pre-incarnate Christ offering salvation through Noah.[21] Following many modern exegetes, I will suggest that Peter does not refer to the *descent* of Christ, but rather the *ascension* of Christ, who proclaims victory over spirits, authorities, and powers.

The phrase *hoti kai Christos* is repeated from 2:21, thus indicating some kind of applicability to the situation of these Christians. In 2:21, it is the exemplary suffering of Christ that is for the benefit of these Christians. Here, the passage serves a dual purpose of not only exhorting these

18. Cited in Achtemeier 1996: 252.
19. For a helpful overview, see Keener 2023: 270-73.
20. Bray 2000: 107.
21. For a rare contemporary proponent of this view, see Grudem 1988: 160.

Christians to carry on doing what is beneficial and good (3:13–17), despite the suffering they are likely to incur, but also to remind them of Christ's victory, which is beneficial and efficacious for them. The use of "because" (*hoti*) at the beginning of the phrase indicates that 3:18–22 serves as the basis for the instructions in 3:13–17. Peter notes that Christ has suffered "once for all" which indicates that his suffering is completed because it has accomplished its purpose. The phrase "suffered for sins" has a sacrificial sense, such as in Hebrews 5:3 and 10:26 (cf. 1 John 2:2).[22] This probably includes all of 2:21–24, including what he suffered before his death. The effect of Jesus' suffering for sins is seen in 4:1–2.

The reminder that Christ "also" (*kai*) suffered for sins provides solidarity to these Christians who are currently suffering. This passage will reframe suffering in the light of eschatological victory. Just as Christ was raised, thus defeating sin and death, they too can have confidence in Christ to defeat death and sin for them. The Messiah is called "the righteous one," which was a significant title in early Christianity denoting Jesus' messianic status and sinless obedience.[23] "It was for them, the formerly unrighteous, that Christ the righteous one died, thus making them righteous as well."[24] Since Christ was himself righteous, he did not need to die for his own sins, he was able to die in the place of others. The innocent one has died in the place of the guilty. There can be no denying some form of substitutionary view of the atonement based on this verse. Williams lays out the case for the various theologies of the atonement the tradition has seen in such passages.[25] Since Peter's purpose is not to expound a particular atonement theory, there are a variety of theological directions such a passage can be taken. Thus, we should keep our attention focused on the specific purpose for which Peter notes such a substitutionary atonement, namely, "in order to bring you to God." Whatever Jesus accomplished on the cross, it was for the purpose of dealing with that which separated the unrighteous from the righteous, and whatever kept the guilty away from the great mercy of God (cf. 1:3).

Peter does not outline any specifics of his atonement theory other than to indicate that the purpose (*hina*) of the life, death, and resurrection

---

22. See also Lev 4:28; 5:7; 6:23; Ps 39:7; Isa 53:5, 10; Ezek 43:21–25.

23. Acts 3:14; 7:52; 22:14; Jas 5:6; 1 John 2:1, 29; 3:7; Diogn. 9:2; Justin Martyr, *Dial.* 17.

24. Achtemeier 1996: 248.

25. Williams 2011: 254–72.

of Jesus was the reconciling of people to God. This can be seen in the parallel passage in 2:25 where the audience is described as those who have "returned to the Shepherd and guardian of their lives." But 2:25 refers to Jesus and not God, which means there is something Trinitarian happening in the logic of this passage as Jesus is the agent who accomplishes reconciliation of those alienated from God the Father, which is also a reconciliation to Jesus.

The Greek phrase (*men . . . de*) creates a contrast that is difficult to translate. We could say that, "even though Jesus was put to death by the flesh," i.e., a reference to his crucifixion by humans, "but" this was overturned and undone by the work of the Spirit, which raised Jesus to life.[26] This fits with the way I understand the dative cases of *sarki* ("flesh") and *pneumati* ("Spirit") being instrumental.[27] This has little to do with the realms or spheres of the flesh vs. the spirit, but rather indicates the specific agents at work here. Jesus was put to death *by* humans and raised to life *by* the Spirit. This is commensurate with other strands of early Christian teaching which indicate that God raised Jesus from the dead (Acts 3:15; 4:10; Rom 10:9; 1 Cor 6:14; Gal 1:1; 1 Thess 1:10), and where Paul indicates the divine agent was the Spirit (Rom 1:4; 8:11).

The logical flow in 3:18–19, from death, through resurrection, to proclamation seems to indicate a sequence of events. This indicates that verse 19 does not refer to the time between Jesus' death and resurrection, since this event happens *after* the resurrection mentioned in verse 18. The opening words of verse 19 *en hō* refer to the means "by which" Jesus "went and made proclamation." This proclamation is announced through the agency of the Spirit.[28] Notice also that we have translated this as "in which he ascended and made an announcement." This suggests that the message was not evangelistic, but rather a declaration to the principalities and powers.[29] Jesus was not seeking to offer anyone salvation through this declaration, but rather seeking to let all the powers of darkness know that God had accomplished

---

26. On the *men . . . de* construction, see Runge 2010: 54–55, 74–83.

27. See Achtemeier 1996: 250.

28. This raises an interesting question with regards to 1 Peter 1:12 ("in regard to the things that have now been announced to you through those who brought you good news by the Holy Spirit sent from heaven"). Does Peter understand this announcement to be done through the Spirit by means of the community? If so, then the church is understood as the couriers of this message of salvation and victory over the enemy (1:12).

29. Paul refers to similar thought in Colossians 2:15, "He disarmed the rulers and authorities and made a public example of them, triumphing over them in it."

his victory, and thus that their time would end soon.[30] This is an important reason for hoping, trusting, and persevering among those who are being harassed as followers of Jesus. These trials will come to an end. Victory is assured because Jesus has conquered the grave and ascended to the right hand of God (3:22).

The "demons in prison" are those spirits that were involved in the evil of humanity during the time of Noah (Jub. 7:21; 1 En. 6–10; 18:12—19:2).[31] The Greek used here is more technically, "spirits," but this very rarely has an anthropological sense (cf. Heb 12:23, where it is clarified by the genitive "just") and commonly is a reference to angels (Heb 1:7, 14) or demons (cf. Matt 8:16; Luke 10:20; 1 John 4:1). That these "spirits" are further described as "in prison" and who were "disobedient" (3:20) indicates their nefarious nature. Therefore, it does not refer to humans. The "prison" refers to a holding place of sorts (cf. 2 Pet 2:4; Jude 6; Rev 20:7). Speculation as to location or specifics of such a prison prove unhelpful at every point. So where did Jesus go? The going of verse 19 probably refers to the same as verse 22 (it is the same word in Greek), where Jesus went to heaven, the dimension of God's manifest presence. This then probably refers to the ascension, much like verse 22 where Peter repeats this thought for emphasis and clarity.

The "spirits" are further described as those who "did not obey," indicating their malevolent nature (cf. 5:8). Their disobedience is the reason for their current imprisonment and Christ's triumphal pronouncement against them. These are the same disobedient spirits that were around during the time of Noah. While the primary context for these verses is 3:18–19 and 22, with the emphasis on the victory and exaltation of Christ, the temporal reference serves to locate the second context for these two verses (20–21), namely, the story of Noah.

These demons were active in the time of Noah, causing destruction and despair for the peoples of the earth. In fact, it is likely that these are the same spirits causing trouble and persecution for these Christians to whom Peter writes (cf. 5:8). These demons are disobedient, just like the people in 2:8. In Genesis 6:3, God is said to have waited 120 years before the judgment of the flood. The reference to God's patience indicates his sovereign care and responsibility to and for creation. God does not delight in judgment

---

30. See Keener 2023: 274–75.

31. While some interpreters reference Genesis 6:1–6, I am not persuaded that this text forms the background to this passage. The language is entirely different and a better interpretation of Genesis 6 is that it refers to the lineage of Seth or perhaps to dynastic rulers of the ancient world.

and death, but rather is patient with a disobedient world, wanting them to respond faithfully to Jesus, who offers them salvation (cf. 2 Pet 3:9).

The story of Noah provides a narrative example of God's patience but also his steadfast judgment. Noah's rescue from the flood (i.e., judgment) provides the interesting analogy with these Christians' situation. By trusting God, Noah built the ark and was saved from impending judgment. Similarly, by trusting Jesus, these Christians are rescued from the judgment that awaits their destructive society. Peter looks to the story of Noah and the flood as a prophetic type (cf. 2 Pet 2:5; 3:6) to use as a foil for his understanding of baptism (3:21). Now, in this phase of God's unfolding drama, these Christians are saved through what baptism indicates. While some older scholars thought of the whole of 1 Peter as a baptismal treatise, that view has rightly not stood the test of time.[32] It is not the baptism that saves them, but rather the devotion to Christ, which baptism symbolizes. Peter is not talking about simply water which washes dirt away, but rather the ritual and symbolic act of Christian baptism which publicly displays one's allegiance to Christ, or what Peter terms "a commitment of a good conscience to God," which indicates a comprehensive allegiance to Christ and his way of life as indicated by the word "faith" or less helpfully, "belief" (*pistis*).

Peter notes that rather than merely functioning as an external cleaning agent, baptism in water indicates the "commitment of a good conscience to God." While the word *eperōtēma* can refer in some situations to a "request" or "response,"[33] in this context it refers to a "pledge" or "commitment."[34] The water in and of itself does nothing. Rather, the ritual of baptism with its communal and theological context is not about washing dirt off the body, but about a symbolic act charged with the meaning of dedicating one's whole self completely and comprehensively to God. The act of baptism is done with an awareness or consciousness of God and God's gracious invitation and gift of new life in Christ. That this is connected to Christ is indicated by the final phrase noting that this is "through the resurrection of Jesus Christ." The resurrection of Jesus is the foundational event upon which faith is based and salvation is received. Baptism is a significant marker and public act of embodied declaration of this commitment to Christ and this is predicated on the victory of God accomplished in and

---

32. For a thorough critique, see Beasley-Murray 1962: 251–58. See also Williams and Horrell 2023: 1:26–27; 1:345–46.

33. BDAG 362.

34. See the discussion in Crawford 2016: 23–37.

through Christ by his resurrection. As Paul would remind us, "if Christ has not been raised, then our proclamation has been in vain and your faith has been in vain" (1 Cor 15:14).

Peter then utilizes a tradition based on Psalm 110:1, namely, the phrase "at the right hand of God," which is also used in Romans 8:34, Colossians 3:1, and Hebrews 10:12. This passage indicates that Jesus has been elevated to a position of unparalleled honor and status.[35] The ascension is indicated again using the same participle as in 3:19 (*poreutheis*). Jesus has ascended into the realm of God's presence where he is seated in the place of supreme authority and honor alongside the Father.

It is not clear whether these three groups of entities ("angels, authorities, and powers") are malevolent or a mixture of good and bad supernatural beings, but regardless, it is clear that all of them are now in subjection to him. It is not clear whether God's vindication and exaltation of the resurrected Jesus subjugates such entities or whether this is done through other means. The point of this passage is that as Christian's face powers and entities that are operative behind and through human structures and persons, the risen Christ can assure them of ultimate victory, despite the current circumstances, which can appear to indicate the opposite.

Peter's audience are facing trials and people are mocking them, as well as ostracizing them socially. This section shows the example of Jesus triumphant over the grave, winning a victory for God, and declaring this victory to the demonic underworld. His ascension to the right hand of God is not a promotion but a vindication of Jesus' true status and position as Lord. And just as Jesus was vindicated by God, so too these Christians will be vindicated and their true status and position will be affirmed as his beloved.

Fusing the Horizon

What can we say to the families of the twenty-one Coptic Christians beheaded in February, 2015? What words of comfort are there for those facing horrendous opposition for their devotion to Jesus? Persecution, social harassment, exclusion are not elements commonly experienced by the majority of Christians in the Western world. But they are a horrific reality for many in other parts of the world. This passage from 1 Peter is perhaps particularly signifi-

---

35. A comprehensive discussion of Psalm 110 and its influence on early Christian thinking is offered by Hengel 1995: 119–225.

cant for them, although it is not insignificant for others. Jesus is able to stand in solidarity with those who suffer. Jesus was despised, rejected, abused, and murdered.[36] We do not serve a Lord unacquainted with grief and sorrow (cf. Isa 53:3). Reflecting on this passage in prayer, I am moved as I consider this quote from John Polkinghorne:

> God is not a spectator, but a fellow-sufferer, who has himself absorbed the full force of evil. In the lonely figure hanging in the darkness and dereliction of Calvary the Christian believes that he sees God opening his arms to embrace the bitterness of the strange world he has made. The God revealed in the vulnerability of the incarnation and in the vulnerability of creation are one. He is the crucified God, whose paradoxical power is perfected in weakness, whose self-chosen symbol is the King reigning from the gallows.[37]

Unimaginable suffering exists in this world. Christ too has suffered in solidarity with his followers. But this passage from Peter offers a deliberate reminder that hope is not a rumor. There will come a time when the ascended Savior announces his final victory, and God will wipe away every tear and heal every sorrow (Rev 21:4). But until that day, we must comfort one another with the solidarity of Jesus' suffering and the hope that his victory over sin and death provides, and we must remain resolute in our commitment to create and sustain communities that embrace his way of life as a beacon of hope to others.[38] Peter's point here is to exhort the church to life in the tension between the already-but-not-yet victory of Christ and how that relates to them as his beloved.

Forsaking a Life of Vice (4:1–6)

> ¹ So, because the Messiah suffered in the flesh, equip yourselves with the same resolve (because the one who has suffered in the flesh is done with sin). ² Do not live by human desires but by the will of God for the rest of your lives. ³ You have wasted enough

36. For a confronting but beneficial reflection on Jesus' abuse, see Tombs 2023.
37. Polkinghorne 1989: 68.
38. An exceptionally helpful theological and pastoral reflection is offered by Swinton 2007.

time doing what pagans like to do, living in depravity, disordered desires, drunkenness, drinking-parties and festivals, and lawless idolatry. **4** They are surprised that you no longer participate in these excesses of degeneracy, and so they blaspheme. **5** But they will answer to the one who is prepared to judge the living and the dead. **6** For this reason the gospel was proclaimed to the dead, in order that, though they had been judged by the flesh, they might live by the Spirit as God does.

This opening verse harks back to the thought of 3:18, which noted the suffering of the Messiah. Since even the Messiah suffered in the flesh, they must likewise be prepared to do so. What does it mean to "equip yourselves also with the same resolve"? And how in fact did Peter imagine his audience doing so? The thought appears to be similar to Philippians 2:5, "have this way of thinking in you which was also in Christ Jesus." The resolve Jesus had when he suffered is to be the same resolve these Christians must have. Jesus was entirely focused on the will of God (4:2), and the joy set before him, namely the liberation of God's people from death, darkness, and despair (2:10). The next part of this verse, "for the one who suffered in the flesh is done with sin," raises several tricky questions: Who is the one who has suffered? Christians or Jesus himself? Following Michaels, I suggest it is Jesus who is being referred to.[39] Jesus has suffered to the extent that sin has been fully dealt with, and now Christians are free to live lives following God's will. Thus, Jesus again becomes the paradigm (2:21) to follow. Since the Messiah has fully dealt with sin, we should also be finished with it. Sin therefore should no longer be a characteristic feature of our lives, since Jesus has suffered for our sin. This follows naturally from the position reached in verse 1. They are willing to suffer for their obedience to the will of God, which suggests they are finished with sin and the damage it brings. Thus, their lives should be shaped not by desires that are characteristic of this world, but by God's desires. Peter is reinforcing their identity as Christians. Following in Jesus' steps involves a total reshaping of life. Where their lives are in sync with the world, change is to occur. God's will must be their focal point and transforming reality.

It seems best to understand the first part of 4:3 as a reference back to 4:2; thus what pagans do is live by mere human desires. In contrast to this, the audience is urged to live not merely by human desires, but by the will of God. This suggests that we are to understand the vice list in 4:3 as

---

39. Michaels 1988: 225–29.

the antithesis of the will of God, actions that go against the calling to be holy (1:15–16) and live honorable lives (2:12). The vices are also illustrative of the kind of life they have forsaken, confirming their identity as former pagans. To engage in these vices would be to conform to previously held ignorant desires (1:14) and would mark a return to futile ways (1:18). Peter underplays his belief that these Christians have spent a *sufficient* or *enough* time (*arketos* is probably an example of meiosis)[40] engaging in activities that reflect selfish-cravings rather than the will of God (4:2).[41] Peter now launches a list of vices that characterize those who live by mere human desires and not by the will of God.[42] The list begins with a *aselgeia*, a word that indicates a "lack of self-constraint which involves one in conduct that violates all bounds of what is socially acceptable."[43] The next vice, "desire" (*epithymia*), can be positive (Luke 22:15; Phil 1:23; 1 Thess 2:17), but while the word is not always negative, in this context it connotes "selfish cravings" or "disordered desires." Next, we have a reference to "drunkenness" (*oinophlygia*), which stands in direct contrast to the exhortation to "sober-mindedness" (1:13; 4:7; 5:8). Clement of Alexandria offers this description of pagan drinking as a warning to Christians.

> But the miserable wretches, who expel temperance from conviviality, think excess in drinking to be the happiest life; and their life is nothing but revel, debauchery, baths, excess, urinals, idleness, drink. You may see some of them, half-drunk, staggering, with crowns around their necks like wine jars, vomiting drink on one another in the name of good fellowship; and others, full of the effects of their debauch, dirty, pale in the face, livid, and still above yesterday's bout pouring yet another bout to last till next morning. It is well, my friends, it is well to make our acquaintance with this picture at the greatest possible distance from it, and to frame ourselves to what is better, dreading lest we also become a like spectacle and laughing stock to others.[44]

The next two vices (*kōmos* and *potos*) have to do with private or public gatherings which contained a variety of elements problematic to those seeking to live holy lives, from various sexual activities, drunken escapades, and

---

40. Achtemeier 1996: 281. See Polybius 1.23.5; 2.27.4.

41. Watson 2012: 97, claims that *arketos* "is used ironically to imply that the time spent doing what the gentiles want is "more than enough."

42. On these vices, particularly idolatry, see du Toit 2021: 421–25.

43. BDAG 141. Similarly, L-N 88.272. See Hobson 2008: 65–74.

44. Clement of Alexandria, *Paed.* 2.2, translation by Elliott 2000: 723.

often included worship of pagan gods (Wis 14:22–27; 2 Macc 6:3–7). Philo uses the same word in a list of activities which he describes as "pursuits of shameful things, an utter destruction and renunciation of what is good, wakefulness during the night for the indulgence of immoderate appetites" (*Cher.* 1.92). The climax of this vice list is "lawless idolatry" (*eidōlolatria*). Beare suggests a link with disgraceful practices linked with certain cults.[45] Michaels suggests that this refers to "something that is utterly inappropriate and repugnant to God."[46] Michaels captures the essence of the word as it is used in a variety of contexts as an action that is deeply offensive and contrary to the way of life established by God. With its connection to idolatry, we have an adjective that describes the range of idolatrous practices as that which is wholly inappropriate for those seeking to conduct themselves according to the will of God.

Their pagan neighbors are "surprised" at the Christian's withdrawal from these particular activities. Does this refer specifically to festivals, feasts, and parties? Achtemeier seems to suggest that we translate the word "taken aback" or "put off," and this would fit the context of social exile well.[47] These unbelievers are shocked and ashamed that these Christians withdraw from pagan festivals, and thus offend not only their friends but also the gods to whom the people pay homage. While *syntrechō* indicates "run together," it is often used as a metaphor for participation. BDAG lists the interpretive option of "to be in harmony with, *agree with*."[48] The phrase here suggests a lack of participation in wretched and wasteful living.

"Flood of immorality" (*asōtia*) may refer back to 3:20, suggesting that the characteristic evil that was part and parcel of Noah's social reality also now pervades the social reality of 1 Peter's audience. A choice is necessitated by these Christians. They cannot hold their allegiance to Jesus and partake of these cultural events. Thus, their allegiance with Jesus brings them into direct disrepute, and they are socially afflicted and condemned.

Blasphemy is a serious offence in Scripture. Friends and family of these followers are so outraged at their behavior that they defame God. One

---

45. Beare 1970: 180.

46. Michaels 1988: 232.

47. Achtemeier 1996: 283. See also Michaels 1988: 233, who notes the parallel in 2 Clem. 17.5.

48. BDAG 976. While used literally in the LXX (Jdt 6:16; 13:13; 14:3; 15:12; 2 Macc 3:19; 6:11), as well as early Christian writings (Mark 6:33; Acts 3:11), it is used more figuratively in the Apostolic Fathers. See 1 Clem. 35.8; Barn. 4.2; Ignatius, *Eph.* 3.2; 4.1; *Pol.* 6.1.

is not sure if this amounts to attacking God directly or indirectly through their attack on Christians. Whichever way one understands this, there will be severe consequences for those who blaspheme, ergo verse 5.

It is not clear as to why they will have to give an account to Jesus. Is it because they engage in these corrupt activities, socially persecute the followers of Jesus, or because they blaspheme? A combination of these factors is enough to invoke divine judgment. "Him" clearly refers to the Father (2:23), the one because of whom they are being socially afflicted. The Father is also the one who will vindicate them and shame their persecutors in judgment because the judgment is based on how one responds to Jesus, as 2:7–8 indicates. The phrase "living and the dead" is a euphemism for everyone that has ever lived. *No one* will escape God's judgment, it applies to every single human being who has ever lived and will ever live.

If the section had ended with verse 5, all would be well. But Peter continues with verse 6, which has proved as difficult to understand as 3:19! Who are the dead to whom Peter refers? And what was preached to them? Does this refer to Christians who have died? Or does it refer to those actually dead having the gospel proclaimed to them? Or is "dead" a metaphor for those spiritually dead? Or does it refer to Christians who have since died? These appear to represent the main exegetical options.[49] Some commentators have connected this to 3:19–20, but Peter uses different language there, and so likely intends something different here. Confidence in one particular interpretation evades this interpreter. It seems unlikely that this refers to Christ preaching the gospel to those who have already died, an idea foreign to early Christianity.[50] Thus, we can either take this as a reference to proclaiming the gospel to those who are spiritually dead (cf. Eph 2:1) or to Christians who have subsequently died. The mention of the "living and the dead" in verse 5, suggests that we understand *nekros* ("dead") as those who have physically died. This could mean that the pastoral situation addressed in this verse is like that of 1 Thessalonians 4:13–18. Have those who turned to Christ in response to the gospel and now have died missed out? Was their fidelity a waste? Peter notes that "they had been condemned in the flesh by human judgment." Society's evaluation of these Christians who had died was simple: they had wasted their lives. "Living for God, following his way of life, and now look at them—they're dead!" But Peter's epistle indicates that human judgments are not God's. That is why he goes on to say,

49. For a detailed discussion, see Horrell 2003: 70–89.
50. See Achtemeier 1996: 289.

that "they might live by the Spirit by God's judgment." God will judge these Christians who have died as faithful, and their inheritance will be secure (1:4). God's Spirit is how life is attained. And these Christians, by trusting Jesus, have gained a relationship with God that will carry them through death and into eternal life, the ultimate vindication for their fidelity.

Life in God's Household (4:7–11)

> ⁷ The climax of everything has drawn near, so exercise self-mastery and be sober-minded for the sake of your prayers. ⁸ As of first importance, maintain eager love for each other, because love deals with a multitude of sins. ⁹ Practice hospitality to one another without criticism. ¹⁰ Because each one of you has received a spiritual gift, minister to one another with it, as beneficial stewards of the varied grace of God. ¹¹ Whoever speaks must do so as one proclaiming the very message of God; whoever ministers must do so with the strength that God provides, so that God may be glorified in all things through Jesus the Messiah. To him belong the glory and the power forever and ever. Amen.

While this section may seem like a tangent to the overall theme of negotiating and navigating life in the Graeco-Roman world as a Christian, this is an integral part of Peter's strategy to aid them. If they are to survive the hostility and suffering imposed by outsiders, then they will need a community that will provide them the necessary comfort, solidarity, and encouragement to remain steadfast in their allegiance to Christ. Thus, this section indicates various points needed to cultivate and sustain their devotion.

Similar to Jesus' announcement that the kingdom of God has "dawned" in Mark 1:15, Peter sounds the clarion call that will awaken those who are idle or not attentive to what God is doing. In 4:7, the word *ēngiken* suggests something drawing so near that its effect is already experienced. Yet what has dawned? Peter says the *telos*, which is *"the last part, close, conclusion, especially of the last things, the final act in the cosmic drama,"*[51] which I have translated as "the climax." The penultimate act of God's redemptive drama has begun with the resurrection of Jesus. The judgment of God is coming, as verse 6 reminds us. This calls for a response from these followers of the Messiah.

---

51. BDAG 998.

An awareness of the "times" creates an intensity/urgency, motivating these followers to seek God regarding how to live, respond, and follow in Christ's "footsteps" (2:21). Peter therefore gives them a vision of the kinds of activities that should characterize their days. Amidst pain and suffering, these followers are reminded to discipline their thoughts (1:13; cf. 5:8). "Self-mastery" is considered one of the cardinal virtues of the Graeco-Roman world. Danker describes this virtue as "a characteristic of those who are in control of their faculties and their responses to stimuli or situations. Such people evoke confidence in their ability to handle crises and make difficult decisions. In a word, they have good judgment."[52] Peter next employs a term related to careful deliberation and thinking with the use of "sober-minded" (1:13; 5:8). They are not to be like drunken people, unaware of their surroundings and predisposed to foolish activities and unwise choices. Rather, their lives are to be intentional and focused on the things of God, lest this hinder their prayers, a feature already noted in 3:7. Self-mastery and sober judgment are required in approaching God and living holy before God. Given that this verse is couched between two sections, one describing their former lives and its consequences (4:1–6) and the next describing intra-communal virtuous living (4:8–11), this verse acts like a bridge by instructing appropriate living before God in either setting.

In a community facing the volatile and uncertain responses of pagans, these Christians must maintain their care, concern, and commitment to one another (v. 8). Love does not refer to a warm, fuzzy feeling, but rather to concrete acts that embody the life-giving example of Jesus (cf. 1 John 3:16). Living together in such communities of mutual concern requires that one be able to deal with infractions and hurts within the community and thus Peter instructs them to love in such a way as to deal with the sins that will inevitably occur. Elliott suggests that "covering" refers to "forgiveness" based on the parallelism of LXX Psalm 31:1 and LXX Psalm 84:3. "As a loving God has covered (forgiven) believers' sins, so they are to cover (forgive) the sins of their brothers and sisters (cf. 1 Cor. 13:7)."[53] This does not entail some facile covering up, but rather the commitment to moral repair of those injured and transformation of those who perpetrate offences, so that they grow from such experiences and learn not to repeat them. The love of God and the Christian community is to bring healing and restoration, not

---

52. Danker 1982: 361. See Plato, *Gorg.* 491D.
53. Elliott 2000: 751.

only to those who sin but also for those who have experienced the harmful effects of the sins of others.

Hospitality is then instructed (v. 9), which was important among early Christians (cf. Rom 12:13; Heb 13:2), even being a necessary mark of healthy leadership (1 Tim 3:2; Titus 1:8). Their identity is to be marked not simply by love but by love working its way through actions of hospitality. They are to *be* hospitable.[54] It is within such hospitable contexts that forgiveness, healing, and transformation will take place. This is an essential aspect of their communal life as well as "a presupposition for the Christian mission."[55]

In verse 10, Peter uses two key words that are usually associated with the Pauline letters, namely "gift" and "ministry." I have chosen to translate the latter word as "ministry" because this is characteristically how the word is used of Christian activity in the New Testament.[56] "Gift" is associated with the spiritual manifestations mentioned by Paul (1 Cor 12 and 14). It is important to note that the variety of gifts, which will be explored in 4:11, have their origin in God's initiative and, furthermore, they are given to each member of the Christian community. Everyone has a gift and a part to play in ministering to others with the gift that they have received. No one is excluded or prioritized in God's gift-giving economy. Therefore "no member can refuse the contribution to the worship or the life of the community which the Spirit would make through him [or her]."[57] And because these are God's gifts, given to God's children, they are to be used to steward God's varied grace to one another. Such gifts are characterized by God's grace and are thus to be beneficial to one another in seeking to live out a holy and christologically shaped life. There are basically two categories of gifts, into which all of them may be divided: speaking and actions (v. 11).[58] The verb *laleō* ("speaking") may thus refer specifically to preaching and teaching[59]

---

54. Cf. Michaels 1988: 247, who argues for an imperatival force. However, Achtemeier 1996: 296 suggests that it is rather descriptive, thus our translation of "being" instead of "be." However, he does acknowledge that the imperatival force is there "but in less blatant form."

55. Goppelt 1993: 299.

56. See Collins 1990.

57. Dunn 1975: 263.

58. Achtemeier 1996: 298.

59. E.g., Acts 2:31; 4:20, 29; 11:14, 15; 1 Cor 2:6, 7; 2 Cor 2:17; 7:14; 12:19; Phil 1:14; Col 4:3; 1 Thess 2:2; Titus 2:15; 2 Pet 1:21; 3:16; cf. Heb 1:1–2; 5:5. I owe this list to Achtemeier 1996: 298n96.

but can also apply to other forms of charismatic utterances.[60] "Whoever speaks must do so as one speaking the very words of God" means that "the content of one's speech must bear the character of God's words and thus the divine intention, not the speaker's own."[61] Peter may thus be both warning and encouraging those who speak to remember that it is *God's* intentions and desires that are of the utmost importance, not what *we* "feel" is important to communicate. Peter instructs that when someone in the community teaches or prophesies, they are in fact representing God. And this should be done prayerfully (v. 7), in love (v. 8), and for the benefit and service of the entire community (v. 10). Those who "minister" (*diakoneō*) are to do so with the enabling of God's strength (*ischys*; cf. Eph 6:10). Here we have an image of reliance upon God to do what God wants to be done. Both speaking and ministering are for the explicit purpose (note the *hina* clause) of bringing glory to God. This provides beneficial criteria with which to determine what kind of speaking and ministering is to be practiced. If it does not ultimately bring glory to God, it is misguided as it misses the point of the gifts of the Spirit. To whom does the glory and power belong? I take this as a direct reference to Jesus the Messiah.[62] First Peter 5:11 and 2 Peter 3:18 indicate this view is consistent with our author's understanding to offer glorious praise to Jesus, the one who is worthy.

Fusing the Horizon

I became a follower of Jesus in October, 1995. Before that, my life was characterized by the vices listed in 1 Peter 4:3. Many of us have had our characters nurtured in contexts of vice and violence. Before following Jesus, one of my favorite places to hang out was at the local bars where they played billiards (eight ball, nine ball, and snooker). Around the table, I was arrogant and rude. I had been playing for a long time and had developed a level of skill that was unhelpful and a magnet for trouble. A lot of my character was both cultivated and displayed around a pool table. The level of my immaturity meant that pool halls and practicing the way of Jesus were in direct competition. I needed to withdraw from such places for a time so that I could heal

---

60. 1 Cor 14:2–3, 27; cf. 1 Cor 12:8–10.

61. Achtemeier 1996: 299.

62. Michaels 1988: 253; Jobes 2005: 283, although see Keener 2023: 333 and Williams and Horrell 2023: 2:405 for the argument that it refers to God.

my character and grow my convictions around Christ. This happened within a Christian community that patiently and gently taught me the way of Jesus as we gathered together and shared our lives. The Christian community provided the context within which to experience authentic hospitality and love, a place I could attend to my many sins and heal the character deficiencies that plagued my relationships. It was among committed Christian community that I was strengthened by the word of God and by the gifts outworked among us. The church is called to be an authentic community where we display our rough edges to one another with the understanding and commitment that this will not be used against us, but will be used to form us as disciples of Jesus and better equip the community on how people need to be loved. Peter outlines a vision of shared responsibility and mutual benefit as each person uses their gifts and talents to further equip, heal, and build the church that can faithfully represent Jesus. Thanks to the church, I can represent Christ in many places, even around a pool table in a bar.

Remain Faithful Even Though It Incurs Suffering (4:12–19)

> 12 Beloved, do not be surprised at the fiery trials that are happening among you, to examine you, as though something odd were happening to you. 13 But, to the extent that you are participating in the Messiah's sufferings, rejoice, so that you may also be glad and shout for joy when his glory is revealed. 14 When you are insulted for the name of the Messiah, you are blessed, because the Spirit of glory, namely, the Spirit of God, is upon you. 15 None of you should suffer for being a murderer, a thief, a criminal, or even a meddler. 16 But when any of you suffers as a Christian, do not consider it shameful, but glorify God in this. 17 For it is time for judgment to begin with the household of God; if it begins with us, what will be the outcome for those who do not obey the gospel of God? 18 And if it is difficult for the righteous to be saved, what will become of the ungodly and the sinners? 19 Therefore, let those suffering, due to obedience to God's will, entrust themselves to a faithful Creator, while continuing to do beneficial deeds.

How did these Christians endure despite social and perhaps even political pressure and especially cultural marginalization? To understand this, we must see how they cultivated their identity and praxis. "Beloved" is a common way to refer to Christians and provides a clear identity marker for God's people.[63] And with this endearing and familial address Peter begins the final section of his letter with some important teaching that would have been as difficult to receive then as it is now. While pagans may be "surprised" at the actions of these Christians (4:4), the latter should not be "surprised" at the tribulations they are currently enduring (i.e., the response of pagans to them). Peter describes this as a "fiery ordeal," an image he has already appealed to in 1:7. Fire can burn, and it can destroy. Fires in Rome were a perpetual threat to the well-being of the people. Cicero viewed fires as one of the great dangers of Roman life (*Off.* 2.19.6). According to Horace, elite Romans feared theft and fires the most (*Sat.* 1.1.77). Then we have the Great Fire of Rome in 64 CE which would have been a harrowing memory for Christians. Tacitus tells us that Christians were used as scapegoats for Nero; they were burned alive or consumed by wild beasts (*Ann.* 15.44.2–5). Thus, for Peter to appeal to the image of a "fiery ordeal" was to tap into an image that many if not most of his audience knew about all too well. The purpose of this tribulation was to test their resolve and character. And this was to be expected, not surprising.

Rather than be caught off guard by their negative experiences of pagan hostility, they should have the perspective of joy as they participate in the Messiah's sufferings. Peter views suffering on account of one's allegiance to Christ, not as something negative, but as something that is good, namely, a joy. This should rightly startle, or should I say provoke, Western Christians. Again, this is not a new thought as Peter has already noted that they are "blessed" to suffer for living just lives according to Christ (3:14; cf. 4:14). Peter is not psychologically unhinged in wanting to suffer, but sees suffering not as something inherently negative if it is caused by living a just life devoted to Christ.

Suffering for one's allegiance and obedience to Christ separates the fans from the followers. The revelation of God's glory when Christ is revealed and the earth is judged will ultimately vindicate them. At the start of verse 14, although the Greek word *ei* can be translated as "if," in this context it should not be understood as a hypothetical scenario. Rather, the force of the conjunction, "combined with a verb in the indicative mood

---

63. Paul refers to individuals as his "beloved" (Rom 16:5, 8, 9, 12; 1 Cor 4:17; Col 1:7; 4:7, 9; Phlm 1, 16), and to his readers as his "beloved children" (1 Cor 4:14), as well as his use of "beloved" as a reference to the whole church (Rom 12:19; 1 Cor 10:14; 2 Cor 7:1; 12:19; Phil 2:12; 1 Thess 2:8).

(*oneidizesthe*), emphasizes the reality of the assumption that Christians will be reproached, and hence has the force not so much of 'if' as of 'when.'"[64] Allegiance to Jesus comes at a cost. Bearing the name of Christ, i.e., "Christian" (cf. 4:16), indicates one's primary loyalty is to Jesus and his community. The idea is similar to what we find in Matthew 5:11–12. Opposition does not necessarily indicate sin or God's displeasure; rather, it is a situation where God can or will be involved. God's presence is assured to those who suffer for the right reasons, i.e., for fidelity to Christ and not because of other reasons (cf. 4:15). The Spirit that testified concerning the sufferings of Christ and was sent to speak to the people of God (1:10–12) is the same glorious Spirit that is with them (cf. Isa 11:2) in their own sufferings.[65] The Spirit provides a foretaste of the eschatological glory they are to receive as those who confess the name of Christ in word and deed.

Peter warns them in 4:15, that if they are to suffer, they should not suffer for sins but rather on account of their righteous lives. They should not suffer for being murderers, thieves, criminals, or mischief makers. We should note that here we have a very pastoral concern for the audiences. If these Christians suffered for their allegiance to Jesus, then the temptation to retaliate would be perpetual. Some of them may even be tempted towards violence in response. Here, Peter's exhortation is for them to avoid such vices and retaliation (cf. 3:9).[66] We should not imagine that Christians were perfect or that somehow such vices were not relevant to them. Given the wide range of Christians addressed (1:1) and that these Christians came from various pagan backgrounds, these instructions would have been necessary. These are realistic instructions for real people facing the ongoing temptation to respond inappropriately to the insults and abuse hurled at them from outsiders.

The conjunction *ei* functions here in 4:16 the same way it did in 4:14, not hypothetically but assuming that the outcome is inevitable; thus I have translated it as "when." This verse provides one of the three times the word "Christian" is used in the New Testament (cf. Acts 11:26; 26:28). Trebilco helpfully notes that the word "Christian" refers to one who belongs to Christ and is an adherent and follower of Christ.[67] "Christian" was used

---

64. Achtemeier 1996: 307.

65. For more on the allusion to Isaiah 11:2, see Jobes 2005: 288.

66. For an in-depth discussion of each of these vices see du Toit 2022: 59–91.

67. Trebilco 2012: 272, "Latinisms like χριστιανός are derived from a proper name or a title. They denote supporters, adherents, followers, or partisans of a person, with the

by outsiders as an insult, intended to shame those who "bear this name." Rather than see this as a stigma, Peter exhorts them to embrace the label Christian as a mark of honor and to glorify God because this is a marker that clearly identifies whom they belong to. They must reframe this insult as a badge of honor and not consider it shameful. After experiencing a humiliating defeat in a public court, Lucius recounts: "On account of my shame, I cannot recall how I washed, how I dried, how I returned home. I was out of my mind, branded and stupefied by the stares, the nods, the pointed fingers of everyone we passed" (Apuleius, *Metam.* 3.12). One can only imagine that this was a regular feature of Christian life for many that Peter wrote to.

Suffering is the reality of these followers now, but judgment (4:17) is coming and has begun with God's people. The notion of judgment here refers to an evaluating process by which people are classed according to their response to Jesus. Those facing suffering now because of Jesus will be found safe from God's final judgment. However, those who reject Jesus, and thus ultimately reject God, will face a severe judgment. Verse 18 forms a parallel to verse 17, repeating the same thought for emphasis. Essentially, Peter is posing the rhetorical question to alert these followers of the worse fate that awaits those who reject Jesus.

In 4:19, Peter concludes the section with an exhortation regarding God's character. We should quickly note, again, that suffering is not the result of God's will, but rather the result of implementing and following God's will. As Achtemeier correctly notes, "Suffering will inevitably result from following God's ways rather than those of secular society."[68] There is at times a marked difference between the ways of God and those of the surrounding culture, bringing those who follow God into conflict with those who do not obey the gospel (v. 18).

Suffering is the natural result of living in an environment hostile to the gospel. Therefore, these Christians (v. 16) are to entrust themselves to the one who is faithful, the Creator. God is utterly faithful to those who belong to him, to those who are his people (2:9). They are valuable and honored by God because they are there for him, and there is a mutual relationship between them and God (1:8). Thus, despite their current situation of suffering, God's faithfulness towards them (1:5) and God's power, illustrated in his ability to create a universe, should provide those suffering persecution

---

key idea conveyed by the suffix being that of 'belonging to' the person to whose name the -ιανός suffix is appended."

68. Achtemeier 1996: 318.

reasons for hope. And reasons for hope (1:3) and trust should encourage them to continue to live "holy lives" that please God.

In fact, the way they are to entrust themselves to God includes their continuing perseverance in doing good. By entrusting themselves to God, they follow the example of Jesus, who also entrusted himself to God (2:23). Jesus entrusted himself to God the judge, who judges justly. And God the judge has vindicated his Son through resurrection and exaltation (3:18–22). The verdict of the powers has been overturned, and the innocent one has been justified. Here, the Christians are exhorted to entrust themselves to God, the faithful Creator. This faithful God is powerful enough to rescue them from the clutches of despair, and even death (5:9).

Social harassment and opposition are not an excuse to stop doing what God has called them to, instead, it is an indication that they are on the right track in following God's will. But what is this "good" that they are called to continue in? Can we be a little more specific? It appears that such "good" would entail holiness and mission. Throughout the letter Peter has advocated the apparent paradox of non-conformity to society's various dark deeds, but continual engagement with society to "win some" (2:12; 3:1–2). Therefore, we may be confident that holiness and mission are the two essential requirements of what it means to live the "good" life.

Fusing the Horizon

The topic of this pericope is suffering and glory, not two words those in the Western world usually associate together. Contemporary Christianity has often drifted into unrealistic and toxic positivity. Brueggemann outlines the issues well when he writes:

> Much of Christian piety and spirituality is romantic and unreal in its positiveness. As children of the Enlightenment, we have censored and selected around the voice of darkness and disorientation, seeking to go from strength to strength, from victory to victory. But such a way ignores the Psalms; it is a lie in terms of our experience. Childs is no doubt right in seeing that the Psalms as a canonical book is finally an act of hope. But the hope is rooted precisely in midst of loss and darkness, where God is surprisingly present. The Jewish reality of exile, the Christian confession of crucifixion and cross, the honest recognition

that there is an untamed darkness in our life must be embraced—all of that is fundamental to the gift of new life.[69]

Jobes rightly draws attention to the constant problem that suffering creates for Christians.[70] It causes us to question where God is and whether we have done something to "deserve" the suffering we are facing. Peter's salutary reminder that allegiance to Jesus can lead to suffering is a message that contemporary Christians need to be regularly reminded of. Too often #blessed is used as marker to indicate some capitalistic notion of material success. Sporting a new pair of Js, getting a new car, or buying a lavish house is no indicator of God's blessing. And we are being betrayed by a brand of Christianity that has confused fame, money, and materialistic success with God's blessing.[71] Success in the Christian life is all about fidelity to God, his people, and his purposes in this world. Those who can remain faithful to Christ amidst the difficulties and sometimes tragedies of life are blessed because they are living God's way but also living into the future that God will ultimately perfect and restore. As our cultures drift further away from the influence of Jesus, it is more and more likely that those desiring to be faithful and holy will inevitably face insults and repercussions. Such a message is not likely to win friends and influence people, but it will differentiate the fans of Jesus from his true followers. In this regard, we have much to learn from sisters and brothers outside the Western world for whom opposition to the faith is more common and at times, as harsh as it was in the first centuries. I am particularly challenged by the words of Wang Yi, who writes: "When you are threatened with death for the gospel, you find out for whom you really live. When faced with the risk of job loss, you know for whom you really work. When you may lose fortune and position for the sake of the gospel, you find out whether you are crazy for money or crazy for the gospel."[72] May the Spirit resting on us remind us whom we belong to and may we ever remain faithful to the Christ who suffered much for us.

---

69. Brueggemann 1984: 11–12.
70. Jobes 2005: 288.
71. See the insightful discussion and critique of Kirby 2021.
72. Yi 2022: 178.

Leaders and Followers in the Household of God (5:1–5)

> ¹ Therefore, as a fellow-leader and a witness of the sufferings of the Messiah, as one who shares in the glory to be revealed, I exhort the leaders among you to ² shepherd the sheep of God among you! Exercise oversight—not under compulsion but willingly, in the manner of God—not for dishonest gain but eagerly. ³ Do not dominate those entrusted to you but be examples to the flock. ⁴ And when the Chief Shepherd appears, you will win the never fading and glorious crown. ⁵ In the same way, the rest of you must submit to the elders. And all of you must clothe yourselves with humility in your dealings with one another, because, "God opposes the proud, and gives grace to the humble."

The author here exhorts those entrusted with the care of God's people. He does not issue a command, but rather appeals to them as one of their own. Peter carefully notes that he too is a fellow elder, probably of the local Christian community in Rome. This indicates his solidarity and shared responsibility to the tasks of leadership and care for the Christian community amidst such perilous circumstances. He does not use his apostolic status, noted in 1:1. Rather, as one who can identify with the specific and challenging needs of the Christian community, Peter alerts them to the fact that he is in the same position they find themselves in. Although Peter was a "witness" to the sufferings of the historical Jesus, "witness" also indicates the notion of "advocate."[73] Peter was not just an arbitrary bystander able to recount certain details of the events. Just as the First Testament prophets testified in advance (1:11), so too Peter testifies retrospectively to the sufferings and death of Jesus. Peter is not only a fellow witness in the sufferings they are currently experiencing, he is also "a partaker of the glory to be revealed." This is a glory that all those who remain faithful to God will participate in (1:21; 4:13–14; 5:10). Glory, a prominent theme throughout this letter (1:7, 11; 4:13–14; 5:1, 4, 10), is the eschatological honor and reward that belongs to those who remain faithful to Jesus.

The word that I have translated "leaders" is usually translated as "elders." But as Green notes, "given the role assumed of these persons in vv. 2–3, I am assuming that 'elders' refers not simply to 'the older people among you' but to leaders who are likely to be drawn from among those

---

73. BDAG 619.

who are older."⁷⁴ Thus, this refers to those who have been identified and/or selected as having mature Christian life-experience, and thus wisdom and the necessary character and convictions to care for God's people. They are specifically exhorted and called upon to shepherd God's flock. The role of shepherding God's people is usually associated with God himself.⁷⁵ God himself is the ultimate Shepherd of his people, and thus any shepherding done by elders is as God's agents of leadership, submitting to God's desires and wishes concerning his people. The calling to lead and oversee God's people is not an easy task. Israel's leaders were also called shepherds, and we know the difficult tasks they had to endure.⁷⁶ There is a twofold task for the shepherd. The internal side includes elements found in Ezekiel 34:4, "You have not strengthened the weak, you have not healed the sick, you have not bound up the injured, you have not brought back the stray, you have not sought the lost." While this portrait is negative, it allows us to see the important elements that are associated with being a shepherd of God's people. All these elements are important when considering the role of leadership amongst these Christians. The external side of this is that, "[Shepherding] is the vigilant attention to threats that can disperse or destroy the flock."⁷⁷ This requires an exercise of values and skills for all sorts of complex and costly occasions and situations, to navigate and negotiate the hostility and opposition faced by these Christian communities. Thus, God promises a true shepherd will arise to care for and lead his people.⁷⁸ Jesus is seen to be that Chief Shepherd in verse 4. This is why Peter reminds them that it is "God's flock" that they are called to care for, protect, and lead. Thus, final accountability is to God, not any human leader or authority figure. This also highlights that the flock are of value because they belong to God. This should always be remembered by elders and those who lead.

It is not clear whether the participle for "exercising oversight" is a secondary activity that leaders are to perform or whether it is how the shepherding activity is to occur.⁷⁹ Either way, Peter is indicating a cluster

74. Green 2007b: 162n25.

75. See Pss 23:1–4; 28:9; 74:1; 77:20; 78:52; 79:13; 80:1; 95:7; 100:3; Isa 40:11; 63:11; Jer 13:17; 23:1–3; 50:6; Ezek 34:6, 8, 31; Mic 7:14.

76. Isa 63:11; Jer 23:4; Ezek 34:23–24; cf. Num 27:17.

77. Laniak 2006: 233.

78. Jer 23:1–4; Ezek 34:23–24; Mic 5:3–5; Zech 10:3; 11:16.

79. See Achtemeier 1996: 325, "The participle [*episkopountes*] is to be construed either as an adverbial participle of attendant circumstance, indicating activity that accompanies and further defines the shepherding ("exercising oversight"), or as an adverbial participle of means, indicating how such shepherding is to occur ('by exercising oversight')."

of activities where care, protection, and leadership of God's people are required. The instruction then moves to a series of qualifying and explicating comments that indicate how leadership is to be exercised amongst the communities. Firstly, leadership is a privilege and something to aspire to (cf. 1 Tim 3:1). Therefore, it is not to be exercised under compulsion or coercion, i.e., leaders should not be forced to be leaders but rather should actively and willingly embrace their positions of responsibility in the community. Given the context of suffering, noted throughout but especially in verse 1, some may have felt pressured to remain leaders and wanted to opt out. Others may have felt pressure to lead due to their circumstances or pressure from others within the community. Still others may have felt tempted to compromise their allegiance to alleviate their suffering. Peter's instruction is that those who lead should not feel they have to but should desire to do so. They should willingly embrace their responsibility with the knowledge that it will be difficult. The second exhortation is to a godly form of leadership, namely, "as God would have you do it." If God was leading these communities, as indeed he is (v. 4), that should shape and determine the style and content of the leadership provided. This recalls the imperative to be holy, as God is holy in 1:16. God's character, concerns, and conduct exhibited in Christ are to be the model for these Christian leaders. Thus leaders, and especially elders in this context, should always ask themselves the question, "Is this the way God wants me to lead his people?" Again, Jesus becomes the exemplary model of what godly leadership entails and looks like. Since Jesus is the embodiment of God, his paradigm becomes the way, the truth, and the life to embrace as leaders in the community. Lastly, Peter warns that leadership is a function within the community that is for the benefit of others, and not for "sordid gain."[80] The phrase is ambiguous, but the intention is clear. The community is the priority, not the elders. Their wants, needs, and desires are to be measured against the needs and issues pertaining to the community. And this should be done with an "eagerness" that demonstrates that leaders have the community as their priority, not their own agenda. There is a consistent concern and emphasis among early Christian writings that leaders should not take advantage of their position.[81] The authority of the gospel held by leaders must be em-

---

80. Laniak 2006: 233: "The abuse of power consistently triggers biblical critiques of leadership that feature the shepherd metaphor." See Ezekiel 34 for a trenchant critique of bad shepherds.

81. See 1 Tim 3:3, 8; Did. 15.1; Pol. *Phil.* 5.2.

bodied in character and praxis. In verse 3, the word *katakyrieuō* indicates *dominion* or *mastery* over someone or something, or to *rule* someone or something.[82] This is a reference to "abusive power" over another and is exactly what should not characterize these leaders. Christian leaders are exhorted not to dominate the church, but to rather live as examples. This suggests that authority and influence are located not in titles or positions of authority but in the integrity and character of the leader's lifestyle, which is the embodiment of their fidelity to Christ. That Peter does not define any specific areas to be modelled by the leaders suggests that they are to be exemplary in all areas of life. Practicing leadership in such a way will win them a glorious crown that will never fade.

In verse 5, *homoiōs* is a transitional device indicating the similarity of the sections related to household duties. Slaves and wives have duties that they must fulfill in order to remain faithful, so too the church has a duty towards Christian leaders as those responsible for their wellbeing and fidelity to God. While the duties envisioned are not the same, since the instructions to slaves and wives are predominantly in the context of relationships to pagans; nevertheless, there is an expectation that Christians will fulfill their duties as part of the Christian community. We could imagine that the elements described in 4:7–11 constitute some of the duties to be fulfilled, as well as aiding other Christians with beneficial works that will help sustain them as they seek to remain faithful. The Christian community as the Spirit's House (2:5) has leaders who are responsible for those within it and those who have duties to them.

My translation of "the rest of you" is based on an interpretive decision. The phrase could be translated "those who are younger," which raises questions: Does this refer to those who are younger in age or in spiritual maturity? If "elders" (5:1, 5) refers to the leaders of the Christian community, does "younger" refer to everyone else? Michaels helpfully draws our attention to the same kind of classification in 1 Clement.

> In 1 Clement, written from Rome a decade or two after 1 Peter (see Introduction), the uprising of "the young against the old" (lit "elders," 3.3; cf. Isa 3:5) is later explained as "the steadfast and ancient church of the Corinthians rebelling against its elders" (1 Clem. 47.6; cf. 44.3–6; see also 54.2b, "only let the flock of Christ have peace with the elders set over it").[83]

---

82. BDAG 519.
83. Michaels 1988: 289.

Therefore, Peter is unlikely addressing those who are young people but rather the rest of the Christian community who were not elders.

Elders have responsibility for the Christian community as shepherds have responsibility for sheep. That entails a certain amount of deference to the care and teaching of the elders from the rest of the Christian community. As the range of issues to be dealt with are complex, Peter appeals to the virtue of humility that should characterize the interactions within the Christian community. However, the location of this instruction on the heels of comments to leaders and the rest of the Christian church indicates that it is particularly the relationship between leaders and the church that is in view. All interactions between leaders and the church are to be shaped by a disposition of humility, and not arrogance. The clothing language indicates that it should be a constant requirement in their interactions. "That Peter would instruct everyone to wear the same garment, irrespective of its color or quality or texture, is itself already a startling negation of the social distinctions that among people in Roman antiquity would have been worn like uniforms in a parade."[84]

The call for humility to characterize their interactions is important as indicated by the appeal to scriptural justification. The *hoti* here can either introduce a quotation or provide the reason ("because"). The quotation is from LXX Proverbs 3:34, with the only difference being the substitution of "Lord" for "God." *Hyperēphanos* refers to those who are "arrogant" or "proud."[85] The reason that they are to embrace humility as the guiding disposition in all their various interactions is that God is actively opposed to the arrogant but gives graciously to the humble. Thinking of one's self as better than others, perhaps displayed in actions of superiority, is unwise as it makes God an enemy. God is seen as an active agent who opposes those who are arrogant, but provides grace to those who imitate Christ's disposition of humility (cf. Phil 2:5–8).

Fusing the Horizon

Every time it happens my heart aches. And it happened again. And it will likely continue to happen again. Another Christian leader or group of leaders caught in the trappings of power have done something unethical, abusive, and

84. Green 2007b: 169.
85. Elliott 2000: 848.

shameful. It is on the secular news.[86] And we should not think this just happens in the megachurches—it happens everywhere. It is just not publicized as much when it happens in the smaller churches. This is why passages like 1 Peter 5:1–5, Ezekiel 34; 1 Timothy 3:1–13, and others are so important for the church and leaders to grapple with. Derek Tidball offers a sobering insight when he writes:

> Even our most well-intentioned acts of service can become infected with the will to exercise power over others. When our service is recognised by others, we easily succumb to the temptation to enjoy the recognition and, even unconsciously, begin to replace the pure desire to serve with the corrupting desire for status.[87]

Some may think that the antidote to this is to have no leadership. But unfortunately, when people try to do this what they inevitably end up with is unaccountable leadership. What we need is a stronger connection of accountability among local leaders and with other external leaders and in our own churches. Leaders are called to shape the ethos and values of our communities, and we need leaders to be chosen not just because they are available or can communicate charismatically, but rather because they have a track record of character and exhibit biblically informed convictions that will stand against the subtle temptations to abuse power and people. You cannot out lead a bad example. And Christian leaders need to be able to lead from their own examples, which requires that the space between leaders and the church must begin to be closed. 1 Timothy 3:2 instructs us that hospitality is a key virtue for Christian leaders, a virtue already highlighted for all Christians in 4:9. Having people in our homes breaks down the dividing walls and allow a mutuality of care, commitment, and concern to be expressed. It allows leaders to be seen as real people, with real families, that are facing the same struggles and issues that everyone else is facing. Having people from the church in our homes allows leaders to be seen not as those on pedestals but as those who are just as vulnerable to temptation and struggles as everyone else. Which is why we need to be praying for those in leadership (cf. 1 Tim 2:1–2) and helping to build strong relationships with them of support and encouragement, but also of gentle correction and critique (cf. 2 Tim 2:24–25) that seeks the best for those who lead and therefore those who are led.

---

86. Examples are endless, but for some recent examples, see Adler 2021; Farrier 2022; Hopkins 2023.

87. Tidball 2008: 189.

Final Exhortations to Trust God Despite Opposition (5:6–11)

6 Therefore, accept your humble status under God's mighty hand, so that he may exalt you at the appropriate time. **7** Throw all your anxiety onto God, because he is concerned about you. **8** Be sober-minded, keep watch. Your enemy, the devil, prowls around like a ferocious lion, looking for someone to devour. **9** Firmly resist him through your fidelity, knowing that your sisters and brothers in all the world are also facing this suffering. **10** And after you have suffered for a little while, the God of all grace, who has called you to his eternal glory in Messiah, will himself restore, support, strengthen, and establish you. **11** To him be the power forever and ever. Amen.

Verse 6 forms a bridge with the preceding section of 5:1–5, where this verse provides a conclusion to what has just been taught.[88] "The focus has shifted from being humble within the community (v. 5) to accepting the humble status forced upon Christians by the rejection and hostility of the surrounding culture (v. 6), a situation faced by all Christians of whom the author is aware (v. 9)."[89] The focal point is again the encouragement of Christians who are attempting to faithfully navigate and negotiate life in relation to pagan society. Peter seeks to remind these Christians that God is committed to them and cares for them (cf. 1:5) because he is good (2:3). Their current situation, difficult as it is, should not lead them to doubt or despair because their future is glorious (1:6–7; 4:13; 5:10). These followers are to embrace and accept their humble position. The instruction to "humble themselves" is drawn from the quotation of LXX Proverbs 3:34 in 5:5, indicating these sections should not be understood as detached from what has preceded. Since God is opposed to the proud, they should not be prideful but accept their humble status. They should do this not only because they do not want God to oppose them, but because God exalts and gives grace to the humble. The theme of humility and exaltation is common to early Christian tradition (Phil 2:8–9; Jas 1:9–11; 4:10) and is an important theme in this epistle (3:18–22).

As those who celebrate and rely on God's power (4:11; 5:11), they must not fight for their honor, but rather come "under the mighty hand of God." This is something that is done continually, not just once. It is a consistent

---

88. Achtemeier 1996: 338.
89. Achtemeier 1996: 338.

Exhortations to Communal Flourishing Amidst Opposition (3:13—5:11) 123

and regular looking to God and trusting God's protection and care. The verse is intended to comfort those suffering from pagan opposition that God will vindicate them at the appropriate time (cf. 4:7, 17). The phrase "mighty hand" is used of God's providential concern and shelter of God's people in the First Testament Scriptures (Exod 3:19; 2 Chr 6:32; Ps 89:13). It is found particularly in reference to the great exodus narrative, but in other references to God's power as well.[90] Peter is exhorting the Christians to trust in God's power and promise that he will deliver them. Exaltation, and thus vindication, will come at the *parousia*, the return of Jesus. History will climax with judgment and restoration, and God's people will be rescued and secured by his awesome power. But until then, these followers are to trust and obey, even through phases of humiliation and suffering. There is no hint here of any arrogance associated with their deliverance. Indeed, any such arrogance would undermine the instruction to accept their humble status. Peter's point is not to cultivate a vindictive response to outsiders because God is mighty and pagans will get what they deserve. Rather, the focus here is on hope for those who are tempted to despair. They must remember and hold onto the fact that they are being protected by the power of God's faithfulness (1:5; 4:19). Christ was devoured by the powerful, but that was no match for God's powerful protection which not only raised Jesus from the dead, but vindicated him to the right hand of God (3:22).

Given the social circumstances of these Christians, the invitation of verse 7 would be a welcomed pastoral note of encouragement. Knowing that God has his mighty hand over them (v. 6), and that God is concerned about them, would provide hope and encouragement to these ostracized ones. One of the ways that their humility can be expressed is in thrusting their cares, concerns, and anxieties upon God in sincere trust that God is able to help. Since God is powerful, they can turn to him for help as they face the trials and turbulences of social opposition (cf. 4:19). The verse reflects a conceptual parallel with Psalm 55:22. Here the Hebrew states: "Throw onto GOD what is given you, and he—he will sustain you. He will never allow the faithful person to fall down."[91] The psalmist is thus encouraging the audience, or author, to take life's experiences that are hard, painful, and unhelpful and to give them over to a God who will provide

---

90. Exod 6:1; 13:3, 9, 14, 16; Deut 3:24; 4:34; 5:15; 6:21; 7:8, 19; 9:26; 11:2; 26:8; 34:12; Ps 135:12; Ezek 20:33–34; Jer 32:21; Dan 9:15.

91. Translation by Goldingay 2007: 177.

deep sustenance. God's protection is promised, and Peter uses this verse to encourage those who may be facing terrible situations. The reason they are to "entrust themselves to the faithful Creator" (4:19) is because God cares. God is not some distant and uninterested deity, but rather the faithful and caring Creator who cares deeply for his people and their plight. Such a capable and competent Creator is able to promise restoration, support, and strength (5:10), so they need not fear or be dismayed.

The word *nēphō* (1:13; 4:7) is a metaphor used to indicate the opposite of incapacitated or intoxicated thinking, and is thus best understood as being "sober-minded."[92] Peter invokes the image of sobriety and watchfulness to instruct them to be consistently on guard and aware of their surroundings (cf. 1:13; 4:7). There is an enemy that lurks, and his mission is to devour them, and Peter's audience should not be naïve or caught off guard. The enemy is titled their "adversary" or "accuser," which is language used in the Hebrew Scriptures to describe "those who opposed God's chosen people."[93] Clearly this is a forceful opposition that affects them and even causes them harm. The second title for this enemy is the usual one, the devil (*diabolos*).[94] "While the opponent is supernatural, his agents are to be thought of here as the human powers who do the bidding of the devil in persecuting Christians."[95] Peter wants to convey a sense of caution about the enemy's abilities and the danger he poses to God's people. This is an enemy that has the power to cause much harm and pain. "The image of a prowling devil suggests that evil is not some impenetrable darkness outside the walls of the church, equally thick in all places; rather, evil is a mobile force, something one always has to deal with but is never quite sure where and how one will encounter it."[96] The devil is an evil enemy that lurks and perverts. An enemy that encourages darkness and damages lives. An enemy that is seeking, hunting, and fighting the people of the world. The constant threat of pagan opposition is not something easily avoided. This opposition could manifest itself in a number of ways from social, to economic, to eventually governmental authorities (cf. Pliny). The site of danger is both

---

92. L-N 30.25. See further Watson 2011: 539–42.

93. Achtemeier 1996: 340. See Isa 41:11; Jer 27:34 (50:34); 28:36 (51:36); Esth 8:11.

94. See Matt 4:5, 8, 11; 13:39; Luke 4:3, 6, 13; 8:12; John 6:70; 1 John 3:8; Rev 2:10; 12:9, 12; 20:2, 10.

95. Achtemeier 1996: 341n66.

96. Volf 1994: 20–21.

the household and public life. Their devotion to Christ and his way of life brings them into an arena of danger that could be deadly.

Rather than abandon their fidelity to Christ and thus the inevitable social opposition that comes from such allegiance, they are to stand their ground and resist the satanic forces that would seek to devour them (v. 9). The word "resist" (*anthistēmi*) refers to an active *resistance* not a passive attitude (cf. Matt 5:39). Similar sentiments are found in James 4:7 and Ephesians 6:11–13. Peter envisions these followers not just passively accepting the destruction caused by their enemy, but rather seeking to engage and stand against their adversary, the devil. The way of resistance is, however, not violent retaliation. The example of Jesus in 2:21–25 would not allow such a response. Rather, they are to stand fast by continuing their trust in Jesus. Resistance is by a continuing allegiance to Jesus and a trusting relationship with him. The fact that Christians "all around the world" are facing similar struggles gives them confidence that what they are facing is not unknown to Christian experience, and they are not isolated in this regard. They stand with many others, a community of God's people, together resisting the forces of darkness.

Despite the violent presence of the enemy noted in 5:8, the gracious God who has called them is able to act for the complete restoration of those who heed his call. The terrifying presence of an enemy who constantly lurks around them in their daily lives cannot and must not give way to doubting the capabilities of the God they have given their lives to. This gracious God who has called them is not only willing, but able to rectify and restore the suffering inflicted upon them by the enemy. While the enemy is acknowledged, the focus of this author is on what God can do, and that is what he seeks to remind these audiences. There are some fascinating contrasts in this verse. Their suffering contrasts with the glory they will receive. Also, the period of suffering is said to be "short" or for a "little while" while the glory is said to be "eternal."[97] Finally, God is named as "the God of all grace," which could suggest various kinds of grace or the totality of grace received by humanity and especially these Christians.

Furthermore, Peter frames the promise of God's restoration with two theological truths that are to sustain them. Firstly, God is gracious. God has a favorable disposition to them and will provide what they need in these perilous times of uncertainty and opposition. Secondly, Christ has called them into God's eternal glory. Such eschatological hope is to inspire

---

97. Achtemeier 1996: 344.

and sustain their fidelity as the suffering they are experiencing is only for a "little while" compared with the hope of "eternal glory." God's grace and hope for the future allow them to be resilient in difficult times. Looking at suffering from a temporal perspective, in the light of an eternal glory, provides perspective that should inform their faithfulness. This climaxes with the comprehensive promise of God that he will restore them, support them, strengthen them, and establish them. In the light of such a hopeful, dare one say wonderful, future outcome, due to the beneficent character of God, the natural response is for Peter to exhort these Christian communities to praise God in the midst of their difficult circumstances (5:11).

Closing Exhortation and Greeting (5:12–14)

> 12 With the help of Silvanus, whom I regard as a trustworthy brother (to you), I have written briefly to exhort you and to testify to you the true grace of God, on which you must stand. 13 Greetings from those in Babylon, chosen together with you, and from Mark, my son. 14 Greet one another with a loving kiss. Peace to all of you in Christ.

The letter is said to have been written "with the help of" or "through" (*dia*) Silvanus. This may indicate that Silvanus was Peter's amanuensis (secretary) or that Silvanus was the bearer of the letter. It is the latter of these two options that many scholars have followed, believing that the episode in Acts 15:22–35 provides an interpretive clue.[98] There Silas travels with others to deliver an apostolic letter to the various churches. The use of "letter-carriers" in early Christianity constitutes an interesting phenomenon, as they were not merely delivery people but were charged with both delivering the message and then clarifying an author's words is greater detail.[99] Thus, it is likely that Silvanus would have travelled to these Christian communities and delivered Peter's "short letter" to these churches, perhaps clarifying anything ambiguous and answering further questions for them related to working out Peter's message in the various locations.

Silvanus was thus a trusted emissary of apostolic leaders, and if he is the same person as the Silas mentioned in Acts 15, then he was a prophetic leader in his own right. Peter probably chose Silvanus due to his familiarity with travelling and relaying apostolic news and teaching. Perhaps, we may

---

98. For discussion, see Richards 2000: 417–41.
99. See Richards 2004: 201–9.

conjecture Silvanus was being trained as an apostle—the tripartite authorship of the Thessalonian correspondence could suggest this (1 Thess 1:1) as well as his inclusion in the group of apostles (1 Thess 2:7). Another reason for thinking this would be that Peter commends Silvanus as a "trustworthy brother." The Greek phrase may indicate that Silvanus was a trustworthy brother "to you" (i.e., the audience), which could indicate a prior relationship that Silvanus had amongst the community. The idea that he is part of those mentioned in 1:12 seems unlikely, for Peter would probably have named Silvanus if that was the case.

The author offers greetings from "those in Babylon." Who is referred to here is unclear, but many think that the church or churches in Rome are in view.[100] The reason Rome is suggested is because "Babylon" is used as a symbolic title for Rome in Jewish and Christian literature. The *Sibylline Oracles* (5.143–68; 5.434), the *Apocalypse of Baruch* (10.1–3; 11.1; 67.7), *4 Ezra* (3.1, 28, 31), and Revelation (14:8; 16:19; 17:5; 18:2–21) also refer to Rome as "Babylon."[101] Ancient textual variants offer "Rome" as a possibility, and indeed scholars have suggested this is the true referent. In Revelation 17:5, the angel shows John a woman with an inscription on her forehead reading: "Babylon the great, mother of whores and of earth's abominations." Babylon clearly held very strong negative connotations for Jews and Christians. So why not just say Rome? Because the metaphor Peter uses describes his situation as well as theirs. Babylon is where the Jews were in exile, and the author of this letter writes from a position of exile to an audience in exile. The world as they know it is far from God's intentions. As Green notes: "This reference to Babylon pulls back the curtain on the real context in which Peter's audience made their lives, focusing attention on the systemic character of harassment and the institutionalization of evil in patterns of sanctioned behavior and organizational structures that legitimate and propagate such behavior."[102] Furthermore, the fall of Babylon was a symbol of God's justice because at one point it was a superpower unrivalled by any other nation, just like Rome in Peter's day. However, by

---

100. The Greek phrase *hē syneklektē* is feminine in gender and thus could be referring to a woman, perhaps Peter's wife. Along with the mention of Mark as Peter's son, this could add to the possibility. However, many ancient manuscripts add the word *ekklēsia* indicating it was understood as referring to a church. Furthermore, the reference in 2 John 13 to the church as the "elect sister" point towards taking this as a reference to the church(es) in Rome.

101. E.g., Isa 13; 43:14; Jer 50:29.

102. Green 2007b: 1.

the time this epistle was written, Babylon was in ruins. Strabo wrote: "The greater part of Babylon is so deserted that one would not hesitate to say.... 'The Great City is a great desert'" (*Geogr.* 16.1.5). Early Christians may have referred to Rome as Babylon to indicate that she too would fail and end up in ruins (cf. Rev 18). And this is exactly what happened. Identifying the church in Rome as "co-elect" reminds the audiences scattered throughout ancient Anatolia that there is a solidarity between them (cf. 1:1; 2:9). All these Christians experience an exilic faith, alienated from the dominant culture by their election to God's people. Just as God's people experienced exile in the First Testament (e.g., 2 Kgs 20:16–18; 24:10–17; Jer 29:1), so too God's people in Peter's day experience the alienating consequences of being God's elect.

It is not clear who "Mark" is or why Peter refers to him as "my son." Is this the same Mark that accompanied Paul? Is this the Mark that authored the Gospel of Mark? We have more questions than our evidence warrants conclusions.

The final verse contains an exhortation to "Greet one another with a loving kiss." The kiss of love is a tangible gesture of relationship that indicates both care and commitment. Kissing was usually reserved for family members, and yet here early Christians utilized this gesture as means of indicating and reaffirming familial connections among themselves (Rom 16:16; 1 Cor 16:20; 2 Cor 13:12; 1 Thess 5:26).[103] Peter has instructed them to "authentic mutual love, love one another deeply from the heart" (1:22), and this gesture is a physical embodiment and practice of such love. The letter ends with a prayer for peace. Peace does not form a dominant theme in the letter (1:2; 3:11; 5:14); however, it is noted at key junctions that frame the discourse. Peace, God's peace, is more than just the absence of angst or conflict. Rather, God's peace is relational and beneficial in all dimensions of life.

Fusing the Horizon

Peter writes within a world that is foreign to the ways of Jesus. He has written an exhortation to these Christians to stand in the truth and grace of God

---

103. It is not clear if there is anything substantially different between Paul's "holy kiss" and Peter's "loving kiss." Perhaps one could suggest that a holy kiss was in some sense distinctive because it is performed in a Christian context, with Christian motivations. But that is perhaps reading too much into the phrase.

despite the opposition and harassment they are currently facing. Those living outside the Western world know all too well the predicament and often pain of fidelity to Jesus. But perhaps, as the influence of Christianity on the Western world fades, those of us residing in the West will also come to realize the difficulties and complexities of our allegiance to Jesus in a world that vies for our attention, affection, and allegiance. Perhaps the influence and persuasion of the Western world will be less violent but influential nonetheless. We are currently being discipled by patterns of thinking and acting in our world that are foreign to the ways of Jesus. Considering this, the ending of Peter's letter seems even more relevant. We must seek out, create, and sustain Christian communities that are attentive to the apostolic witness of Scripture. It is only by deeply attending to the word of God in Scripture that we will have hope to stand fast in the grace of God. Being formed in the ways of Jesus does not happen by accident or mere circumstance. Rather, following Jesus necessitates intentional connection and devotion to the ways of Jesus learned, practiced, and sustained in communities of faithfulness that deeply reflect on the message and significance of Scripture. Being Christians requires an attentiveness to the wider body of Christ so that we may learn together and mutually benefit one another through authentic Christian relationships and edification. It is only by pursuing Christ, in community, that we will be able to testify appropriately to others the wonderful and restorative grace of God found in the gospel of Christ and the transformative life offered to all by the Spirit. In a sense, the ending of this letter provides an apt challenge to those who claim the name "Christian" to live out that message and participate in God's mission for reconciliation and restoration of God's beautiful but fractured world. It is in this way that we will experience the deep and abiding peace of Christ individually and communally, as well as share that peace with others.

BIBLIOGRAPHY

Achtemeier, Paul J. 1996. *1 Peter: A Commentary on First Peter*. Hermeneia. Minneapolis: Fortress.
Adler, Dan. 2021. "Carl Lentz Accused of Repeated Sexual Abuse by Hillsong Pastor." *Vanity Fair*, June 1. https://www.vanityfair.com/style/2021/06/carl-lentz-abuse-allegations.
Agnew, Francis H. 1983. "1 Peter 1:2: An Alternative Translation." *CBQ* 45: 68–73.
Allison, Dale C. 1985. *The End of the Ages Has Come: An Early Interpretation of the Passion and Resurrection of Jesus*. Philadelphia: Fortress.
Balch, David L. 1981. *Let Wives Be Submissive: The Domestic Code in 1 Peter*. SBLMS 26. Chicago: Scholars.
———. 1986. "Hellenization/Acculturation in 1 Peter." In *Perspectives on First Peter*, edited by C. H. Talbert, 79–101. Macon, GA: Mercer University Press.
Balz, Horst Robert, and Gerhard Schneider, eds. 1990. *Exegetical Dictionary of the New Testament*. 3 vols. Grand Rapids: Eerdmans.
Barclay, J. M. G. 1993. "Conflict in Thessalonica." *CBQ* 55: 512–30.
Barr, A. 1961–62. "Submission Ethic in the First Epistle of Peter." *Hartford Quarterly* 2: 27–33.
Bates, Matthew W. 2017. *Salvation by Allegiance Alone: Rethinking Faith, Works, and the Gospel of Jesus the King*. Grand Rapids: Baker Academic.
Bauckham, Richard. 1988. "Pseudo-Apostolic Letters." *JBL* 107: 469–94.
———. 1997. "James, 1 Peter, Jude and 2 Peter." In *A Vision for the Church: Studies in Early Christian Ecclesiology in Honour of J. P. M. Sweet*, edited by M. Bockmuehl and M. B. Thompson, 153–66. Edinburgh: T&T Clark.
Bauer, Walter. 2000. *A Greek–English Lexicon of the New Testament and Other Early Christian Literature*. 3rd ed. Edited by W. F. Arndt et al. Chicago: University of Chicago Press.
Bauman-Martin, Betsy J. 2004. "Women on the Edge: New Perspectives on Women in the Petrine Haustafel." *JBL* 123: 253–79.
Beare, Francis W. 1970. *The First Epistle of Peter*. Oxford: Blackwell.
Beasley-Murray, G. R. 1962. *Baptism in the New Testament*. Grand Rapids: Eerdmans.
Bechtler, Steven Richard. 1998. *Following in His Steps: Suffering, Community, and Christology in 1 Peter*. SBLDS 162. Atlanta: Scholars.
Best, Ernest. 1970. "1 Peter and the Gospel Tradition." *NTS* 16: 95–113.
Blundell, Mary Whitlock. 1989. *Helping Friends and Harming Enemies: A Study in Sophocles and Greek Ethics*. Cambridge: Cambridge University Press.

Bockmuehl, Markus. 2012. "Hope and Optimism in Straitened Times." *Pro Ecclesia* 21: 7–24.
Boring, M. Eugene. 1999. *1 Peter*. ANTC. Nashville: Abingdon.
Brandt, Wilhelm. 1953. "Wandel als Zeugnis nach dem 1. Petrusbrief." In *Verbum Dei manet in aeternum*, edited by W. Foerster, 10–25. Witten: Luther-Verlag.
Bray, Gerald, ed. 2000. *James, 1–2 Peter, 1–3 John, Jude*. ACCS 11. Downers Grove, IL: IVP.
Brooke, Alan E. 1912. *A Critical and Exegetical Commentary on the Johannine Epistles*. ICC. London: T&T Clark.
Brower, Kent E. 2005. *Holiness in the Gospels*. Kansas City: Beacon Hill.
Brueggemann, Walter. 1984. *The Message of the Psalms: A Theological Commentary*. Minneapolis: Augsburg.
Caird, G. B. 1994. *New Testament Theology*. Completed and edited by L. D. Hurst. Oxford: Clarendon.
Campbell, Douglas A. 2020. *Pauline Dogmatics: The Triumph of God's Love*. Grand Rapids: Eerdmans.
Christensen, Sean. 2018. "Reborn Participation in Christ: Recovering the Importance of Union with Christ in 1 Peter." *JETS* 61: 339–54.
Cicero, Marcus Tullius. 1930–2010. *Orations*. Translated by John H. Freese et al. 11 vols. LCL. Cambridge: Harvard University Press.
———. 1999. *On the Commonwealth and On the Laws*. Edited by James E. Zetzel. Cambridge: Cambridge University Press.
———. 2003. *Topica*. Edited with a translation introduction, and commentary by Tobias Reinhardt. Oxford: Oxford University Press.
Cohick, Lynn H. 2009. *Women in the World of the Earliest Christians: Illuminating Ancient Ways of Life*. Grand Rapids: Baker.
Collins, John N. 1990. *Diakonia: Re-interpreting the Ancient Sources*. Oxford: Oxford University Press.
Cranfield, C. E. B. 1954. *The First Epistle of Peter*. London: SCM.
Crawford, Matthew R. 2016. "'Confessing God from a Good Conscience': 1 Peter 3:21 and Early Christian Baptismal Theology." *JTS* 67: 23–37.
Danker, Fredrick W. 1982. *Benefactor: Epigraphic Study of a Graeco-Roman and New Testament Semantic Field*. St. Louis: Clayton.
Daube, D. 1947. "Κερδαίνω as a Missionary Term." *HTR* 40: 109–20.
Davids, Peter H. 1990. *The First Epistle of Peter*. NICNT. Grand Rapids: Eerdmans.
———. 2004. "A Silent Witness in Marriage: 1 Peter 3:1–7." In *Discovering Biblical Equality: Complementarity Without Hierarchy*, edited by R. W. Pierce and R. M. Groothuis, 224–38. Downers Grove, IL: IVP.
Delling, Gerard. 1964–76. "ὑποτάσσω." In *Theological Dictionary of the New Testament*, edited by Gerhard Kittel and Gerhard Friedrich, translated and edited by G. W. Bromiley, 8:39–46. 10 vols. Grand Rapids: Eerdmans.
deSilva, David A. 2004. *An Introduction to the New Testament: Contexts, Methods & Ministry Formation*. Downers Grove, IL: IVP.
de Ste Croix, G. E. M. 1963. "Why Were the Early Christians Persecuted?" *Past and Present* 26: 6–38.
Dickson, John P. 2003. *Mission-Commitment in Ancient Judaism and in the Pauline Communities*. Tübingen: Mohr Siebeck.
———. 2021. *Bullies and Saints: An Honest Look at the Good and Evil of Christian History*. Grand Rapids: Zondervan.

Dubis, Mark. 2002. *Messianic Woes in First Peter: Suffering and Eschatology in 1 Peter 4:12–19*. New York: Lang.

———. 2010. *1 Peter: A Handbook on the Greek Text*. BHGNT. Waco, TX: Baylor University Press.

Duke, R. K. 2003. "Priests, Priesthood." In *Dictionary of the Old Testament: Pentateuch*, edited by T. Desmond Alexander and David W. Baker, 646–55. Downers Grove, IL: IVP.

Dunn, James D. G. 1975. *Jesus and the Spirit: A Study of the Religious and Charismatic Experience of Jesus and the First Christians as Reflected in the New Testament*. London: SCM.

du Toit, Sean. 2016. "1 Peter and Negotiating Life in the Graeco-Roman World." PhD diss., University of Otago.

———. 2019. "Negotiating Hostility Through Beneficial Deeds." *Tyndale Bulletin* 70: 221–43.

———. 2021. "Practicing Idolatry in 1 Peter." *JSNT* 43.3: 411–30.

———. 2022. "Ethical Lists in 1 Peter." *JGRChJ* 18: 59–91.

———. 2023. "Honor and Reciprocity in 1 Peter." *BBR* 33: 55–75.

Elliott, John H. 1966. *The Elect and the Holy: An Exegetical Examination of 1 Peter 2:4–10 and the Phrase βασίλειον ἱεράτευμα*. NovTSup 12. Leiden: Brill.

———. 1990. *A Home for the Homeless: A Social Scientific Criticism of 1 Peter, Its Situation and Strategy*. Minneapolis: Fortress.

———. 2000. *1 Peter*. AB 37B. New York: Doubleday.

Farrier, David. 2022. "Hillsong Isn't the Only Abhorrent Megachurch." *Webworm with David Farrier*, April 4. https://www.webworm.co/p/arise?s=w.

Forbes, Greg W. 2014. *1 Peter*. Exegetical Guide to the Greek New Testament. Nashville: B&H Academic.

Garnsey, Peter, and Richard Saller. 1987. *The Roman Empire: Economy, Society, and Culture*. London: Duckworth.

Goldingay, John. 2007. *Psalms 42–89*. Volume 2. Grand Rapids: Baker.

Goppelt, L. 1993. *A Commentary on 1 Peter*. Translated by J. E. Alsup. Grand Rapids: Eerdmans.

Green, Joel B. 2007a. "Living as Exiles: The Church in the Diaspora in 1 Peter." In *Holiness and Ecclesiology in the New Testament*, edited by K. E. Brower and Andy Johnson, 311–25. Grand Rapids: Eerdmans.

———. 2007b. *1 Peter*. THNT. Grand Rapids: Eerdmans.

Grudem, Wayne. 1988. *1 Peter*. TNTC. Leicester: IVP.

———. 1991. "Wives Like Sarah, and the Husbands Who Honor Them: 1 Peter 3:1–7." In *Recovering Biblical Manhood and Womanhood: A Response to Evangelical Feminism*, edited by John Piper and Wayne Grudem, 194–208. Wheaton, IL: Crossway.

Guder, Darrell L. 2003. "From Mission and Theology to Missional Theology." *Princeton Seminary Bulletin* 24: 36–54.

Gundry, R. H. 1967. "'Verba Christ' in 1 Peter: Their Implications Concerning the Authorship of 1 Peter and the Authenticity of the Gospel Tradition." *NTS* 13: 336–50.

Gupta, Nijay. 2013. "What Is in a Name? The Hermeneutics of Authorship Analysis Concerning Colossians." *CBR* 11: 196–217.

Harris, Murray. 1999. *Slaves of Christ: A New Testament Metaphor for Total Devotion to Christ*. Downers Grove, IL: IVP.

Hartog, Paul. 2014. "The Maltreatment of Early Christians: Refinement and Response." *SBJT* 18: 49–79.
Hauerwas, Stanley, and William H. Willimon. 1989. *Resident Aliens: Life in the Christian Colony*. Nashville: Abingdon.
Hengel, Martin. 1981. *Judaism and Hellenism: Studies in their Encounter in Palestine during the Early Hellenistic Period*. Translated by John Bowden. Minneapolis: Fortress.
———. 1995. *Studies in Early Christology*. Edinburgh: T&T Clark.
Hillyer, Norman. 1971. "'Rock-Stone' Imagery in 1 Peter." *TynBul* 22: 58–81.
Hobson, G. Thomas. 2008. "ασέλγεια in Mark 7:22." *FN* 21: 65–74.
Holloway, Paul A. 2009. *Coping with Prejudice: 1 Peter in Social Psychological Perspective*. WUNT 244. Tübingen: Mohr Siebeck.
———. 2011. "1 Peter and Prejudice." *Sewanee Theological Review* 54: 199–220.
Hopkins, Keith. 1978. *Conquerors and Slaves*. Cambridge: Cambridge University Press.
Hopkins, Rebecca. 2023. "2 Megachurches Rocked by Allegations They Allowed Pastor Guilty of Clergy Sexual Abuse to Re-Offend." *The Roys Report*, February 27. https://julieroys.com/two-megachurches-rocked-allegations-allowed-pastor-guilty-clergy-sexual-abuse-re-offend/.
Horrell, David G. 1997. "Whose Faith(fulness) Is It in 1 Peter 1:5?" *JTS* 48: 110–15.
———. 2003. "Who Are 'The Dead' and When Was the Gospel Preached to Them? The Interpretation of 1 Pet 4.6." *NTS* 48: 70–89.
———. 2007. "Between Conformity and Resistance: Beyond the Balch-Elliott Debate Towards a Postcolonial Reading of First Peter." In *Reading First Peter with New Eyes: Methodological Reassessments of the Letter of First Peter*, edited by Robert L. Webb and Betsy Bauman-Martin, 111–43. London: T&T Clark.
———. 2008. *1 Peter*. London: T&T Clark.
———. 2009. "Aliens and Strangers? The Socioeconomic Location of the Addressees of 1 Peter." In *Engaging Economics: New Testament Scenarios and Early Christian Reception*, edited by Bruce W. Longenecker and Kelly D. Liebengood, 176–202. Grand Rapids: Eerdmans.
———. 2013. *Becoming Christian: Essays on 1 Peter and the Making of Christian Identity*. LNTS 394. London: Bloomsbury.
Hunter, James Davison. 2010a. *To Change the World: The Irony, Tragedy, and Possibility of Christianity in the Late Modern World*. Oxford: Oxford University Press.
———. 2010b. "Interview with Christopher Benson." *Christianity Today*, May, 2010. http://www.christianitytoday.com/ct/2010/may/16.33.html.
Imes, Carmen. 2023. *Being God's Image: Why Creation Still Matters*. Downers Grove, IL: IVP.
Jeremias, Joachim. 1967. *The Prayers of Jesus*. London: SCM.
Jobes, Karen H. 2003. "The Syntax of 1 Peter: Just How Good is the Greek?" *BBR* 13: 159–73.
———. 2005. *1 Peter*. BECNT. Grand Rapids: Baker Academic.
Judge, Edwin A. 2010. "The Quest for Mercy in Late Antiquity." In *Jerusalem and Athens: Cultural Transformation in Late Antiquity*, edited by Alanna Nobbs, 185–97. Tübingen: Mohr Siebeck.
Justin Martyr. 2003. *Dialogue with Trypho*. Translated by T. B. Falls. Revised with a New introduction by T. P. Halton. Edited by M. Slusser. Washington, DC: Catholic University of America Press.
Keener, Craig S. 2023. *1 Peter: A Commentary*. Grand Rapids: Baker.

Kiley, Mark. 1987. "Like Sarah: The Tale of Terror behind 1 Peter 3:6." *JBL* 106: 689–92.

Kinzig, Wolfram. 2021. *Christian Persecution in Antiquity*. Translated by Markus Bockmuehl. Waco, TX: Baylor University Press.

Kirby, Ben. 2021. *PreachersNSneakers: Authenticity in an Age of For-Profit Faith and (Wannabe) Celebrities*. Nashville: Thomas Nelson.

Kroeger, Catherine Clark. 2004. "Toward a Pastoral Understanding of 1 Peter 3.1–6 and Related Texts." In *A Feminist Companion to the Catholic Epistles and Hebrews*, edited by Amy-Jill Levine with Maria Mayo Robbins, 82–88. London: T&T Clark.

Laniak, Timothy S. 2006. *Shepherds After My Own Heart: Pastoral Traditions and Leadership in the Bible*. Downers Grove, IL: IVP.

Lieu, Judith M. 2004. *Christian Identity in the Jewish and Graeco-Roman World*. Oxford: Oxford University Press.

Marshall, Christopher. D. 2001. *Beyond Retribution: A New Testament Vision for Justice, Crime, and Punishment*. Grand Rapids: Eerdmans.

———. 2012. *Compassionate Justice: An Interdisciplinary Dialogue with Two Gospel Parables on Law, Crime, and Restorative Justice*. Eugene, OR: Cascade.

Marshall, I. H. 1991. *1 Peter*. IVPNTC. Downers Grove, IL: IVP.

Martin, Troy W. 1999. "The TestAbr and the Background of 1 Pet 3:6." *ZNW* 90: 139–46.

McKnight, Scot. 2004. "Aliens and Exiles: Social Location and Christian Vocation." *WW* 24: 378–86.

Meade, D. G. 1986. *Pseudonymity and Canon*. WUNT 39. Tübingen: Mohr.

Michaels, J. Ramsey. 1988. *1 Peter*. WBC. Waco, TX: Word.

Misset-van de Weg, Magda. 2004. "Sarah Imagery in 1 Peter." In *A Feminist Companion to the Catholic Epistles and Hebrews*, edited by Amy-Jill Levine with Maria Mayo Robbins, 50–62. London: T&T Clark.

Mitchell, C. W. 1987. *The Meaning of BRK "To Bless" in the Old Testament*. Atlanta: Scholars.

Mitchell. Stephen. 1993. *Anatolia: Land, Men, and Gods in Asia Minor*. Vol. 2, *The Rise of the Church*. Oxford: Clarendon.

Neyrey, Jerome H. 1998. *Honor and Shame in the Gospel of Matthew*. Louisville: Westminster John Knox.

Nietzsche, Friedrich. 2002. *Beyond Good and Evil*. Edited by Rolf-Peter Horstmann and Judith Norman. Translated by Judith Norman. Cambridge: Cambridge University Press.

Oakes, Peter. 2001. *Philippians: From People to Letter*. SNTSMS 110. Cambridge: Cambridge University Press.

Pahl, Michael W. 2006. "The 'Gospel' and the 'Word': Exploring Some Early Christian Patterns." *JSNT* 29: 211–27.

Pate, C. Marvin, and Douglas W. Kennard. 2003. *Deliverance Now and Not Yet: The New Testament and the Great Tribulation*. New York: Lang.

Peeler, Amy. 2022. *Women and the Gender of God*. Grand Rapids: Eerdmans.

Polkinghorne, John. 1989. *Science and Providence: God's Interaction with the World*. London: SPCK.

Richard, E. J. 2000. *Reading 1 Peter, Jude, and 2 Peter: A Literary and Theological Commentary*. Macon, GA: Smyth and Helwys.

———. 2004. "Honorable Conduct Among the Gentiles—A Study of the Social Thought of 1 Peter." *WW* 24: 412–20.

Richards, E. Randolph. 2000. "Silvanus Was Not Peter's Secretary: Theological Bias in Interpreting διὰ Σιλουανοῦ . . . ἔγραψα." *JETS* 43: 417–41.

———. 2004. *Paul and First-Century Letter Writing: Secretaries, Composition, and Collection*. Downers Grove, IL: IVP.

Riddell, Mike. 1998. *Threshold of the Future: Reforming the Church in the Post-Christian West*. London: SPCK.

Robinson, Olivia F. 2007. "The Role of Delators." In *Beyond Dogmatics: Law and Society in the Roman World*, edited by J. W. Cairns and P. J. du Plessis, 206–20. Edinburgh: Edinburgh University Press.

Rosner, Brian. 2013. *Paul and the Law: Keeping the Commandments of God*. Downers Grove, IL: IVP.

Runge, Steven E. 2010. *Discourse Grammar of the Greek New Testament: A Practical Introduction for Teaching and Exegesis*. Peabody, MA: Hendrickson.

Saller, Richard P. 1997. *Patriarchy, Property, and Death in the Roman Family*. Cambridge: Cambridge University Press.

Schelkle, K. H. 1988. *Die Petrusbriefe, der Judasbrief*. Freiburg: Herder.

Schertz, Mary H. 1992. "Nonretaliation and the *Haustafeln* in 1 Peter." In *The Love of Enemy and Nonretaliation in the New Testament*, edited by W. H. Swartley, 258–86. Louisville: Westminster/John Knox.

Schreiner, Thomas R. 2003. *1, 2 Peter, Jude*. NAC. Nashville: Broadman & Holman.

Schrenk, Gottlob. 1964–76. "Γράφω, Γραφή, Γράμμα, Ἐγγράφω, Προγράφω, Ὑπογραμμός." In *Theological Dictionary of the New Testament*, edited by Gerhard Kittel and Gerhard Friedrich, translated and edited by G. W. Bromiley, 1:772. 10 vols. Grand Rapids: Eerdmans.

Schüssler-Fiorenza, Elisabeth. 1983. *In Memory of Her: A Feminist Theological Reconstruction of Christian Origins*. New York: Crossroad.

Schutter, W. L. 1989. *Hermeneutic and Composition in First Peter*. WUNT II/30. Tübingen: Mohr Siebeck.

Seland, Torrey. 2005. *Strangers in the Light: Philonic Perspectives on Christian Identity in 1 Peter*. Leiden: Brill.

———. 2009. "Resident Aliens in Mission: Missional Practices in the Emerging Church of 1 Peter." *BBR* 19: 565–89.

———. 2013. "Crucial Issues in the Quest for the First Readers of 1 Peter." In *Bedrängnis und Identität. Studien zu Situation, Kommunikation und Theologie des 1. Petrusbriefes*, edited by D. du Toit and T. Jantsch, 43–58. Berlin: de Gruyter.

Selwyn, Edward G. 1950. "The Persecutions in 1 Peter." *BSNTS* 1: 39–50.

———. 1964. *The First Epistle of St. Peter: The Greek Text with Introduction, Notes, and Essays*. 2nd ed. New York: St. Martin's.

Senior Donald P., and Daniel J. Harrington. 2003. *1 Peter, Jude and 2 Peter*. SP 15. Collegeville, MN: Liturgical.

Senior, Donald, and Carroll Stuhlmueller. 1983. *The Biblical Foundations for Mission*. New York: Orbis.

Sly, Dorothy I. 1991. "1 Peter 3:6b in the Light of Philo and Josephus." *JBL* 110: 126–29.

Smith-Christopher, Daniel L. 2002. *A Biblical Theology of Exile*. Minneapolis: Fortress.

Spencer, Aída Besançon. 2000. "Peter's Pedagogical Method in 1 Peter 3:6." *BBR* 10: 107–19.

Spicq, Celas. 1994. *Theological Lexicon of the New Testament*. Translated and edited by James D. Earnest. Peabody, MA: Hendrickson.

Stackhouse, John G. 2000. *Humble Apologetics: Defending the Faith Today*. Oxford: Oxford University Press.
Swanson, Dwight D. 2007. "Holiness in the Dead Sea Scrolls: The Priorities of Faith." In *Holiness and Ecclesiology in the New Testament*, edited by Kent E. Brower and Andy Johnson, 19–39. Grand Rapids: Eerdmans.
Swinton, John. 2007. *Raging with Compassion: Pastoral Responses to the Problem of Evil*. Grand Rapids: Eerdmans.
Talbert, Charles H. 2007. *Ephesians and Colossians*. Grand Rapids: Baker Academic.
Tàrrech, Armand Puig i. 2008. "The Mission According to the New Testament: Choice or Need?" In *Einheit der Kirche im Neuen Testament: Dritte europäische orthodox-westliche Exegetenkonferenz in Sankt Petersburg, 24–31. August 2005*, edited by A. A. Alexeev et al., 231–47. Tübingen: Mohr Siebeck.
Tellbe, Mikael. 2009. *Christ-Believers in Ephesus: A Textual Analysis of Early Christian Identity Formation in a Local Perspective*. WUNT 242. Tübingen: Mohr Siebeck.
Thompson, James W. 1966. "Be Submissive to Your Masters: A Study of 1 Peter 2:18–25." *Restoration Quarterly* 9: 66–78.
Tidball, Derek. 2008. *Ministry by the Book: New Testament Patterns for Pastoral Leadership*. Nottingham: Apollos.
Tombs, David. 2023. *The Crucifixion of Jesus: Torture, Sexual Abuse, and the Scandal of the Cross*. London: Routledge.
Trebilco, Paul. 2007. *The Early Christians in Ephesus from Paul to Ignatius*. Grand Rapids: Eerdmans.
———. 2014. *Self-Designations and Group Identity in the New Testament*. Cambridge: Cambridge University Press.
Van der Toorn, Karel. 2007. *Scribal Culture and the Making of the Hebrew Bible*. Cambridge: Harvard University Press.
van Rensburg, F. J. 2009. "No Retaliation! An Ethical Analysis of the Exhortation in 1 Peter 3:9 Not to Repay Evil with Evil." In *Animosity, the Bible, and Us: Some European, North American, and South African Perspectives*, edited by John T. Fitzgerald et al., 199–230. Atlanta: SBL.
van Unnik, Willem C. 1980. "The Redemption in 1 Peter I 18—19 and the Problem of the First Epistle of Peter." In *Sparsa Collecta*, Part II, 3–82. Leiden: Brill.
Vanhoozer, Kevin J. 2005. *The Drama of Doctrine: A Canonical Linguistic Approach to Christian Theology*. Louisville: Westminster John Knox.
Volf, Miroslav. 1994. "Soft Difference: Theological Reflections on the Relation Between Church and Culture in 1 Peter." *Ex Auditu* 10: 15–30.
Warden, P. Duane. 1986. "Alienation and Community in 1 Peter." PhD diss., Duke University.
Watson, Duane F. 2011. "Spiritual Sobriety in 1 Peter." *ExpTim* 122: 539–42.
Watson, Duane F., and Terrance Callan. 2012. *First and Second Peter*. Paideia. Grand Rapids: Baker.
Wells, Jo Bailey. 2000. *God's Holy People: A Theme in Biblical Theology*. Sheffield: Sheffield Academic Press.
Westfall, Cynthia L. 2011. "Running the Gamut: The Varied Responses to Empire in Jewish Christianity." In *Empire in the New Testament*, edited by Stanley E. Porter and Cynthia Long Westfall, 230–58. Eugene, OR: Pickwick.
Williams, Martin. 2011. *The Doctrine of Salvation in the First Letter of Peter*. SNTSMS 149. Cambridge: Cambridge University Press.

Williams Travis B., and David G. Horrell, 2023. *1 Peter: A Critical and Exegetical Commentary*. Vol. 1, *Chapters 1–2*. ICC. London: T&T Clark.

———. 2023. *1 Peter: A Critical and Exegetical Commentary*. Vol. 2, *Chapters 3–5*. ICC. London: T&T Clark.

Williams, Travis B. 2012a. "Suffering from a Critical Oversight: The Persecutions of 1 Peter Within Modern Scholarship." *CBR* 10: 275–92.

———. 2012b. *Persecution in 1 Peter*. NovTSup 145. Leiden: Brill.

———. 2014. *Good Works in 1 Peter*. WUNT 337. Tübingen: Mohr Siebeck.

Winter, Bruce W. 1988. "The Public Honoring of Christian Benefactors: Romans 13:3–4 and 1 Peter 2:14–15." *JSNT* 34: 87–103.

Witherington, Ben, III. 2008. *Letters and Homilies for Hellenized Christians*. Vol. 2, *A Socio-Rhetorical Commentary on 1–2 Peter*. Downers Grove, IL: IVP.

Woan, Susan. 2004. "The Psalms in 1 Peter." In *The Psalms in the New Testament*, edited by Steve Moyise and Maarten J. J. Menken, 213–29. London: T&T Clark.

Wolterstorff, N. 2008. *Justice: Rights and Wrongs*. Princeton: Princeton University Press.

Wright, N. T. 1992. *The New Testament and the People of God*. London: SPCK.

Yi, Wang. 2022. *Faithful Disobedience: Writings on Church and State from a Chinese House Church Movement*. Edited by Hannah Nation and J. D. Tseng. Nottingham: IVP.

INDEX

References following "n" refer notes.

abusive power, 119
agathopoieō, 92
agathos, 92
amanuensis, 1–2, 126
anastrophē, 92
angels, 26, 98
anger, 79
apotithēmi, 42
arrogance, 120, 123
aselgeia (lack of self-constraint), 103
atonement, 47, 69, 71, 96
    ethical component to, 71
    substitutionary, 71, 96
audience, 4–6, 13, 23, 70, 100, 102, 127
    as gentile converts, 6
    as God's chosen instruments, 15
    as obedient children, 29–30
    as powerless and without legal recourse, 8
    situation, 6–10
    See also Christians
authorship, 1–4
    pseudonymity, 1, 3
    Van der Toorn on, 2–3

Babylon
    fall of, 127–28
    Jews and, 127
baptism, 99–100
beneficial deeds, 62, 93–95
blasphemy, 104–5
blessing, 86–87

"calling," 51, 87
canonical competence, 73, 73n73
chosen exiles, 13–16, 46, 55
chosen race, 49–50
Christians
    baptism, 99–100
    as criminals, 56
    duties, 61, 119
    faithfulness (*See* faithfulness)
    holy living (*See* holy living)
    humble status, 122
    Peter's vision of life, 15–16 (*See also* life)
    prosecution of, 8–9
    as slaves (*See* slaves/slavery)
    sufferings (*See* sufferings)
    as a third race, 50
    See also God; Jesus
church, 11, 45, 54, 73, 110, 120–21, 126, 127
    as bearer of divine presence, 49
    mission of, 52
civic authorities, 62
compassion, 17–19
concord, 85
conversion, 40, 72
    corporate dimension of, 51
    mutual love and, 41
corporate testing, 7, 21
corporate worship, 51
covering. *See* forgiveness

date (of 1 Peter), 4
deceit, 42, 43
demons, 98–99
depravity, 42, 43
desires, 6, 30, 103
    ignorant, 32–33, 103
destiny, 48–49
devil, 124, 125. *See also* enemy
discipline, 29
drunkenness, 103

eidōlolatria. *See* lawless idolatry
enemy, 124–25
    resistance to, 125
ēngiken, 106
envy, 42–43, 43n47
eperōtēma, 99
epistrephō, 72. *See also* conversion
epopteuō, 56, 58, 59
eschatology, 38
ethics, 57–60
ethnos, 50
eusplanchnoi, 85
evil deeds, 42–43
evil-speech, 43
exile(s)
    chosen, 13–16, 46, 55
    defined, 55
    social, 104

faith, 8, 10–11, 20, 49, 99
    exilic, 128
    opposition to, 115
    resurrection and, 99
faithfulness, 6, 11, 14, 16, 20–23, 26–27, 38, 69, 72, 110–15, 116, 119, 123–26
faithful presence, 77, 77n86
flood of immorality, 104
foreknowledge, 15, 38
forgiveness, 107
freedom, 62–63
fulfillments, 23–27

gentleness, 79, 91, 92
gifts, 108–9
Gladiator, 39

glory, 116
    sufferings *vs.*, 125–26
God
    awareness of, 44
    as benevolent benefactor, 21
    chosen people, 14, 16, 55, 124
    compassion of, 17–19
    divine initiative, 15
    faithfulness (*See* faithfulness)
    as the Father, 29–30, 36, 37
    fidelity to, 21
    foreknowledge, 15
    glorifying, 59, 59n18
    grace of, 24, 29, 43–44
    as a higher master, 67
    as impartial judge, 35–39
    as judge, 114
    light of, 51
    mercy, 51–52
    mighty hand of, 122–23
    mission and message of, 73
    patience of, 98–99
    power of, 11, 113, 122–23
    restorative justice, 11
    as a rock, 45
    roles and responsibilities, 72
    as Shepherd of his people, 117
    trusting protection and care of, 122–26
    will of, 93, 102–3
    word of, 43–44
good works. *See* beneficial deeds
guile, 69–70
gynaikeios, 82

healing, 71–72
hoi ándres, 82
holiness, 30–35
    as communal accountability, 35
    as a distinctive way of life, 50
    as followers of Jesus, 34–35
    as separation, 31–34
holy kiss, 128n103
holy living, 74–89
    avoiding vices (*See* vices)
    character and conduct, 78–79
    characteristics, 84–89

men, 82–84
wives, 74–76
women (*See* women)
See also sacrifices
Holy Spirit, 15–16, 24, 25–26
holy women, 79–82
homoiōs, 119
honorable conduct, 54–60, 92–93
    concept, 55–56
    ethical witness, 56–57
    reason for, 56
honor/honoring, 63–64, 83–84
hope
    fulfillment of, 23–27
    living, 17–20, 21, 43, 45
hospitality, 108
hostile curiosity, 60, 90, 91–92
humbleness, 85, 122
humility, 120, 122
hypakouō, 80–81. *See also* obedience
hyperēphanos, 120
hypocrisy, 42, 43
hypotassō, 61

identity, 31, 33, 44, 49–50, 103, 108
    audience (*See* audience)
    as chosen exiles, 14, 46, 55
    markers, 46, 49, 111
    social, 94
    superordinate, 50, 52
idolatry, 6, 37, 56, 60, 93, 104
ignorance, 6, 18, 30, 31, 51, 62
imperatival force, 108n54
improvisation, 73
inheritance, 19–20, 41
insincerity, 42
integrity, 76–77
    defined, 76
    faithful presence, 77
Israel, 13–14, 41, 49
    as chosen nation, 14
    holy women, 79–82
    sacrificial cult, 38

Jesus
    ascension, 46, 98, 100
    baptism and, 99–100
    as Chief Shepherd, 72, 117
    death of, 27, 28, 38, 46, 71, 95, 96–97
    embracing paradigm of, 72–74
    entrusted himself to God, 114
    example of, 68–72
    fidelity to, 21, 22
    first followers of, 13
    grace, 28–29
    as a living stone, 19, 45–46
    love for, 22
    as Messiah, 13, 38
    obedience to, 15
    perfect life of, 38
    pre-existence of, 38
    as pre-existent, 24
    proclamation, 97–98
    resurrection of, 17, 19, 21, 22, 24, 27, 28, 38, 95, 96–97, 99–100, 106, 114
    revelation of, 29, 30, 38
    as righteous one, 96
    sacrifices, 16, 37–38, 71
    teachings of, 86
    transformative gospel of, 72
Jews, 5–6, 127
joy, 21
    of actualization, 27
    of anticipation, 27
    perspective of, 111
judgment, 113
    eschatological, 57
    of God, 35–40, 57, 98–99, 106
    sober, 107

kiss/kissing, 128
kyrios, 80, 81

lack of self-constraint. *See aselgeia* (lack of self-constraint)
laleō, 108–9
lawless idolatry, 104. *See also* idolatry
leaders/leadership, 72, 116–21
    defined/described, 117
    duties, 119
    exercising oversight, 117–18
    Green on, 116–17

leaders/leadership (*cont.*)
  holding authority of the gospel, 118–19
  as shepherds, 117
  suffering, 118
  willingly embracing position of, 118
liberation
  from meaningless ways of life, 33, 37
  as ransom, 37
  salvation as, 37
life, 15
  example of Jesus, 68–72, 95–101
  fulfilling one's duty, 60–64
  honorable conduct, 54–60, 92–93
  as a household-slave (*See* slaves/slavery)
  See also holy living
light, 51
living hope, 17–20, 21, 43, 45
love, 64, 107–8
  mutual, 39, 40–41, 42

mataios, 6, 37
men, 82–84. *See also* holy living
mental vigilance, 33
ministry, 108, 109
mission, 57–60
missionaries, 25, 30

nēphō, 124
new birth, 19, 49, 72
Noah, 98–99

obedience, 80–82
  as an integral aspect discipleship, 40
  embodying, 40
  to truth, 40, 41
  See also women
oiketai, 66. *See also* slaves/slavery

pagan(s)
  idolatry, 6, 37, 56, 60, 93, 104
  immorality, 6
  negotiating life among (*See* life)
  opposition to (*See* sufferings)
  slaves of (*See* slaves/slavery)
  wives of (*See* wives)

pastoral sensitivity, 85
patroparadotos, 37
peace/peacefulness/peacemaking, 79, 87–88, 128
peirasmos, 7
persecution, 4, 5, 7–9, 11, 98, 113–14
phobos, 91. *See also* reverence
positive self-concept, 94
prautēs, 91. *See also* gentleness
priests, 50
prison, 98
promiscuous woman, 78
prophets, 23–27, 41, 116
psychē, 23, 55
purity, 40, 75
  goal of, 40

resistance, 125
restoration, 123, 125–26
resurrection of Jesus, 17, 19, 21, 22, 24, 27, 28, 38, 95, 96–97, 99–100, 106, 114
revenge, 79, 85–86
reverence, 67, 75, 91, 92
Rome, 127, 128

sacrifices, 50
  cultic, 9, 36
  Jesus, 16, 37–38, 71
  spiritual, 47
salvation, 17–18, 19, 20, 23–26, 38, 42, 44, 91, 99
  benefits of, 87
  eschatological, 21–23, 71
  as liberation, 37
sanctification, 15
self-concept, 94
self-mastery, 107
Silas, 126
Silvanus, 14–15, 126–27
sin, 51, 68, 69, 96
  power of, 71
  purification of, 71
  See also holiness
slaves/slavery, 10, 64–67
  in ancient world, 64
  duties, 66, 67, 119

Index   143

as irrational brutes, 66
as speaking tools, 64
treatments, 66–67
sober judgment, 107
sobriety, 29, 33, 124
social exile, 104
social harassment, 4, 7–10, 93, 114
  agents of, 10
  reason for, 9
speaking, 108–9
spirits, 98
spiritual house/household, 46–47, 49
spiritual sacrifices, 47
subsequent glory, 24
substitutionary atonement, 71, 96
sufferings, 7–10, 110–15
  allegiance to Jesus leading, 9, 104, 111–12, 115
  as blessing, 91
  of Christ, 7–8, 95–96, 101, 102, 112, 116
  glory *vs.*, 125–26
  God's will and, 113
  judgment and, 113
  period of, 125
  persecution (*See* persecution)
  social harassment (*See* social harassment)
  unimaginable, 101
superordinate identity, 50, 52
sympathy, 85
syneidēsis, 66

telos, 106
tender-heartedness, 85

testing, 7, 20–23
  corporate, 7, 21
  tribulation, 21–22, 111
tribulation, 21–22, 111
trust, 122–26
truth
  concept, 40
  obedience to, 40, 41, 42

verbal abuse, 9, 43, 70, 91
vices, 6, 42–43, 55, 56, 103–5
virtues, 84–89
vision of the Christian life, 15–16

wickedness, 42
wives, 10, 74–76
  duties, 119
  missional (married to pagan husbands), 74–75
  purity, 75
  reverence for God, 75
women
  character and conduct, 78–79
  clothing/dressing, 78, 79
  cultural pressures, 79
  holy, 79–82
  Juvenal on, 78
  promiscuous, 78
  treatment with honor, 84
  as vessels, 83
  weakness and weaker social position, 83–84
word(s), 88–89
  of God, 43–44
worship, 50–51
  corporate, 51

AUTHOR INDEX

Achtemeier, Paul J., 1, 4, 6, 8, 10, 14, 32, 36–44, 49, 51, 57, 61–64, 67, 70, 75, 82–84, 91–92, 95–97, 103–5, 108–9, 112–13, 117, 122, 124–25
Adler, Dan, 121
Agnew, Francis H., 16
Allison, Dale C., 7

Balch, David L., 10, 34, 51, 76
Balz, Horst Robert, 65
Barclay, J. M. G., 7
Barr, A., 61
Bates, Matthew W., 20
Bauckham, Richard, 1, 3, 47
Bauman-Martin, Betsy J., 10, 67
Beare, Francis W., 20, 57, 58, 104
Beasley-Murray, G. R., 99
Bechtler, Steven Richard, 8, 62
Best, Ernest, 57, 58
Blundell, Mary Whitlock, 86
Bockmuehl, Markus, 19
Boring, M. Eugene, 10, 28, 46, 67, 69
Brandt, Wilhelm, 57
Bray, Gerald, 95
Brooke, Alan E., 39
Brower, Kent E., 32
Brueggemann, Walter, 114, 115

Caird, G. B., 11
Callan, Terrance, 91
Campbell, Douglas A., 89
Christensen, Sean, 49
Cicero, Marcus Tullius, 2, 85, 111
Cohick, Lynn H., 78

Collins, John N., 108
Cranfield, C. E. B., 24, 83
Crawford, Matthew R., 99

Danker, Fredrick W., 107
Daube, D., 75
Davids, Peter H., 7, 46, 48, 51, 79, 80, 83
de Ste Croix, G. E. M., 7
Delling, Gerard, 61
deSilva, David A., 9
Dickson, John P., 59, 73
du Toit, Sean, 1, 21, 37, 45, 56, 63, 76, 84, 85, 87, 91, 93, 94, 103, 112
Dubis, Mark, 7, 45, 57, 82
Duke, R. K., 50
Dunn, James D. G., 108

Elliott, John H., 1, 4–6, 10, 13, 24, 32, 34, 37, 47, 49–51, 57, 58, 66, 83, 86, 87, 93, 103, 107, 120

Farrier, David, 121
Forbes, Greg W., 33

Garnsey, Peter, 7
Goldingay, John, 123
Goppelt, L., 8, 14, 49, 51, 57, 66, 83, 108
Green, Joel B., 1, 31, 32, 33, 34, 38, 41, 66, 67, 71, 75, 87, 116, 117, 120, 127
Grudem, Wayne, 80, 95
Guder, Darrell L., 77
Gundry, R. H., 58
Gupta, Nijay, 2

Harrington, Daniel J., 83
Harris, Murray, 63
Hartog, Paul, 11
Hauerwas, Stanley, 77
Hengel, Martin, 32, 100
Hillyer, Norman, 47
Hobson, G. Thomas, 103
Holloway, Paul A., 8, 9, 66
Hopkins, Keith, 64, 65
Hopkins, Rebecca, 121
Horrell, David G., 1, 4, 6, 13, 14, 19, 20, 25, 40, 49, 52, 62, 70, 93, 94, 99, 105, 109
Hunter, James Davison, 77

Imes, Carmen, 35

Jeremias, Joachim, 7
Jobes, Karen H., 1, 29, 30, 43, 59, 67, 68, 70, 72, 73, 80, 91, 109, 112, 115
Judge, Edwin A., 18

Keener, Craig S., 29, 36, 38, 47, 95, 98, 109
Kennard, Douglas W., 7
Kiley, Mark, 81
Kinzig, Wolfram, 11, 56
Kirby, Ben, 115
Kroeger, Catherine Clark, 61

Laniak, Timothy S., 117, 118
Lieu, Judith M., 4

Marshall, Christopher. D., 11
Marshall, I. H., 1, 25, 26, 47
Martin, Troy W., 80
McKnight, Scot, 6
Meade, D. G., 3
Michaels, J. Ramsey, 4, 46, 57, 58, 66, 71, 79, 81, 86, 91, 92, 102, 104, 108, 109, 119
Misset-van de Weg, Magda, 81
Mitchell, C. W., 87
Mitchell. Stephen, 6, 9

Neyrey, Jerome H., 64
Nietzsche, Friedrich, 77

Oakes, Peter, 8

Pahl, Michael W., 75
Pate, C. Marvin, 7
Peeler, Amy, 18
Polkinghorne, John, 101

Richard, E. J., 58, 61
Richards, E. Randolph, 1, 126
Riddell, Mike, 35
Robinson, Olivia F., 9
Rosner, Brian, 26
Runge, Steven E., 97

Saller, Richard, 7
Saller, Richard P., 65
Schelke, K. H., 80
Schertz, Mary H., 10
Schneider, Gerhard, 65
Schreiner, Thomas R., 65
Schrenk, Gottlob., 69
Schüssler-Fiorenza, Elisabeth, 8
Schutter, W. L., 8
Seland, Torrey, 4, 58, 59
Selwyn, Edward G., 7, 9, 24, 48, 58, 85
Senior, Donald P., 59, 83
Sly, Dorothy I., 81
Smith-Christopher, Daniel L., 14
Spencer, Aída Besançon, 61
Spicq, Celas, 55, 61
Stackhouse, John G., 76, 77
Stuhlmueller, Carroll, 59
Swanson, Dwight D., 32
Swinton, John, 101

Talbert, Charles H., 2
Tàrrech, Armand Puig i., 92
Tellbe, Mikael, 4, 5
Thompson, James W., 61
Tidball, Derek, 121
Tombs, David, 101
Trebilco, Paul, 4, 59, 112

Van der Toorn, Karel, 2, 3
van Rensburg, F. J., 5
van Unnik, Willem C., 5
Vanhoozer, Kevin J., 73

Volf, Miroslav, 93, 124

Warden, P. Duane, 5
Watson, Duane F., 91, 103, 124
Wells, Jo Bailey, 32, 33
Westfall, Cynthia L., 82
Williams, Martin, 96
Williams, Travis B., 1, 4–6, 8, 9, 13, 14, 19, 25, 40, 49, 62, 93, 94, 99, 109

Willimon, William H., 77
Winter, Bruce W., 57, 93
Witherington, Ben, III, 5, 24, 26, 67
Woan, Susan, 47, 48
Wolterstorff, N., 36
Wright, N. T., 7, 25

Yi, Wang, 115

ANCIENT DOCUMENT INDEX

HEBREW BIBLE/OLD TESTAMENT

Genesis
1:27	34
6:1–6	98
6:3	98
12:1–3	14, 87
12:7–8	36
12:13	81
14:20	18
16:2	81
18:12	80
18:12–13	80
18:19	15
19:2	80
20:5	81
20:13	81
21:10–12	81
21:12	81
22:1	7, 21
23:4	13
23:6	80
24:27	18
31:35	80
33:8	80
33:11	87
42:10	80

Exodus
3:19	123
6:1	123
12:11	29
13:3	123
13:9	123
13:14	123
13:16	123
15:25	7, 21
16:4	7, 21
18:10	18
19:5–6	49
19:6	34
23:22	34
34:6	18

Leviticus
4–6	71
4:28	96
4:31	71
4:35	71
5:7	96
5:10	71
5:13	71
5:16	71
5:18	71
6:7	71
6:23	96
16	71
17:7	37
19	31
19:2	31, 32, 80
20:7	80
20:26	80
21:8	80
25:23	13

Numbers

27:17	117

Deuteronomy

3:24	123
4:28	45
4:34	123
5:15	123
6:21	123
7:6–13	34
7:8	123
7:19	123
9:26	123
11:2	123
24:17	36
26:8	123
27:19	36
28:36	45
28:64	45
29:17	45
30:1–10	19
32:4	45
32:5	65
34:12	123

1 Samuel

25:27	87

2 Samuel

23:3	45

2 Kings

19:18	45
20:16–18	128
24:10–17	128

1 Chronicles

29:15	13

2 Chronicles

6:32	123

Esther

8:11	124

Job

20:29	72

Psalms

1:3	45
2:3	45
2:4	45
18:2	45
19:14	45
23:1–4	117
28:9	117
31:1	107
33:9	44
33:13–17	87
34:8	44
39:7	96
39:12	13
55:22	123
62:3	45
70:22	30
74:1	117
77:20	117
77:41	30
78:52	117
79:13	117
80:1	117
84:3	107
88:19	30
89:13	123
95:7	117
100:3	117
116:4	36
116:17	36
118	51
119:19	13
119:105	51
135:12	123

Proverbs

2:13	51
3:34	122
5:5	122
16:28	65
18:21	88

Isaiah

1:4	30
1:17	36
2:8	47
3:5	119
5:16	30
6:10	72
9:1	51
11:2	112
12:6	30
13	127
14:27	30
17:7	30
26:4	45
28:16	47
28:19	23
29:23	30
30:12	30
30:15	30
30:18	18
30:29	45
37:19	45
40:6	23
40:11	117
40:25	30
41:11	124
43:14	127
43:19–21	49
45:11	30
49:13	18
53	70
53:3	101
53:4	68
53:5–6	72
53:5	68, 96
53:6	68
53:7	37, 68
53:8	68
53:9	23, 68, 69
53:10	96
53:12	68
54:10	18
55:5	30
60:1	51
63:7	18
63:11	117

Jeremiah

1:5	15
2:7	19
2:27	45
3:9	45
8:19	37
10:15	37
10:25	6
13:17	117
23:1–4	117
23:3–6	72
23:4	117
27:34	124
28:36	124
29:1	128
31:10	72
32:21	123
50:6	117
50:29	127
50:34	124
51:36	124

Lamentations

5:2	19

Ezekiel

20:33–34	123
34	118, 121
34:4	117
34:6	117
34:8	117
34:11	72
34:23–24	72, 117
34:31	117
37:24	72
43:2	51
43:21–25	96

Daniel

9:15	123

Hosea

2:23	51
13:5	15

Joel

2:32	36

Amos

3:2	15

Micah

5:3–5	117
7:14	117

Zechariah

7:9–10a	36
10:3	117
11:16	117

NEW TESTAMENT

Matthew

4:5	124
4:8	124
4:11	124
5:10	93
5:11–12	112
5:12	21
5:14–16	59
5:16	57, 58, 59
5:38–44	86
5:39	125
5:44	86
6:9	36
6:13	7
7:24–27	48
8:16	98
10:25	69
11:29	79
13:17	24
13:39	124
26:4	42
26:53	70
26:67	65

Mark

1:15	106
6:33	104
7:22	42
8:34–38	69
10:16	86
10:38–39	69
13:32	26
14:1	42
14:27–28	69
14:36	36
14:58	46
14:65	65
15:29	46

Luke

1:47	21
2:51	61
4:3	124
4:6	124
4:13	124
6:27–28	86
6:28	86
8:12	124
10:20	98
10:21	21
11:4	7
12:11–12	91
12:35–36	29
15:10	26
16:13	66
21:12–16	69
22:15	103
22:28–30	7
24:50	86

John

1:47	42
2:19	46
3:3–5	19
5:35	21
6:70	124
8:56	21
15:16	14

Acts

2:26	21
2:31	108
2:40	65

Ancient Document Index

3:11	104	14:22	91
3:14	96	16:5	111
3:15	97	16:8	111
3:19	72	16:9	111
4:10	97	16:12	111
4:20	108	16:16	128
4:29	108	16:25–26	26
7:52	96		
7:58	42		

1 Corinthians

2:6	108
2:7	108
3:16–17	46
4:12	86
4:14	111
4:17	111
6:14	97
6:19	46
7:12–16	33
9:3	91
9:19–22	75
10:14	111
12	108
12:8–10	109
13:7	107
14	108
14:2–3	109
14:27	109
14:32–40	61
15:14	100
16:13	91
16:16	61
16:20	128

9:3	51
9:35	72
10:7	66
11:14	108
11:15	108
11:21	72
11:26	112
13:10	42
14:15	37, 72
15	126
15:22–35	126
17:30	30
22:1	91
22:14	96
25:16	91
26:18	51
26:28	112

Romans

1:4	97
1:29	42
2:7	22
6:11	71
6:13	71
6:18	71
8:11	97
8:15	36
8:34	100
8:39	62
10:9	97
12:2	30
12:9	42
12:13	108
12:14	86
12:17	86
12:19	111
13:12–13	42
14:4	66

2 Corinthians

2:17	108
5:17	19
5:21	69
6:6	42
6:16	46
7:1	111

2 Corinthians (cont.)

7:11	91
7:14	108
12:16	42
12:19	108, 111

Ephesians

2:1	105
2:19–22	46
4:1–3	86
4:2	91
4:18	6, 30
4:25–32	42
4:31	42
4:32	85
5:21	61
6:9	65
6:10	109
6:11–13	125

12:20 — 43
13:12 — 128

Galatians

1:1	97
4:6	36
4:8–10	6
4:8–9	30
5:23	91

Philippians

1:11	22
1:14	108
1:23	103
2:2	85
2:5	102
2:5–8	120
2:8–9	122
2:12	111
2:15	65

Colossians

1:7	111
1:23	62
3:1	100
3:8	42
3:12	91
3:13	86
4:1	65
4:3	108
4:7	111
4:9	111

4:16 — 18

1 Thessalonians

1:1	127
1:6	7
1:9	72
1:10	97
2:2	108
2:3	42
2:7	127
2:8	111
2:17	103
3:3	7
3:3–5	7
3:7	7
4:5	30
4:13–18	105
5:15	86
5:26	128
5:27	18

2 Thessalonians

1:4	7
1:6	7
3:12	79

1 Timothy

1:5	42
2:1–2	121
2:2	79
3:1	118
3:1–13	121
3:2	108, 121
3:3	118
3:15	46

2 Timothy

1:5	42
2:24–25	121
4:16	91

Titus

1:8	108
2:5	61
2:10	59

2:15	108	1:3	19, 29, 33, 45, 49, 50, 51, 69, 72, 73, 91, 96, 114
3:5–6	19	1:4	19, 41, 87, 106
		1:5	71, 72, 91, 113, 122, 123

Philemon

1	111	1:6–9	17, 20, 32
16	111	1.6–7	5, 122
		1:6	7, 20, 21, 22, 44

Hebrews

1:1–2	108	1:7	29, 111, 116
1:7	98	1:8	21, 44, 64, 113
1:14	98	1:9	23
3:6	46	1:10–12	17, 23–27, 32, 41, 112
4:13	62		
4:15	69	1:11	7, 24, 116
5:3	96	1.12	57
5:5	108	1:12	30, 32, 72, 97, 126–28
7:26	69		
10:12	100	1:13–21	32, 40
10:21	46	1:13–18	55
10:26	96	1:13–16	28–31
10:34	85	1:13—2:10	28–31
12:1	42	1:13—2:3	33
12:18–24	46	1:13	32, 33, 91, 103, 107, 124
12:23	98		
13:2	108	1:14	6, 32, 33, 37, 40, 41, 62, 103
		1:15–16	32–34, 41, 43, 47, 50, 55, 56, 73, 75, 80, 93, 103

James

1:9–11	122		
1:18	19	1:15	30, 32, 51, 55, 69
1:21	42	1:16	32, 34, 118
3:17	42	1:17–21	35–38
4:7	125	1:17	13, 20, 21, 29, 33, 37, 50, 55, 67, 91
4:10	122		
5:6	96	1:18–19	37, 47, 50, 51
		1:18	6, 30, 33, 45, 55, 60, 63, 72, 103

1 Peter

1:1–2	13–16	1:19–20	24
1:1	3, 5, 6, 13, 25, 49, 50, 112, 116, 128	1:19	47
		1:20	24, 37
1:2	18–20, 23, 29, 33, 34, 40, 42, 46, 48, 73, 128	1:21	38, 91, 116
		1:22–25	39–41, 42
		1:22	23, 33, 34, 42, 43, 64, 128
1:3–5	17, 32		
1:3–4	21	1:23–25	42
1:3–12	17, 28, 47	1:23	19, 43, 45, 49, 50, 51, 72, 73

1 Peter (cont.)

1:24–25	23
1:25b	48
2:1–3	41–44, 53
2:1	42–44, 55, 70–72, 74, 84, 93
2:2–3	42
2:2	20, 42, 44
2:3	41, 45, 52, 122
2:4–10	14, 44–52
2:4	19, 47
2:5	19, 32, 34, 45, 86, 119
2:6–7	47
2:6	23
2:7–8	105
2:8	98
2:9–12	33
2:9–10	6, 15, 47, 51, 75
2:9	32, 34, 46–51, 86, 87, 113, 128
2:10	102
2:11–12	42, 54–57
2:11—4:11	54
2:11—3:12	54–89
2:11	13, 23, 33, 37
2:12	8, 10, 21, 22, 33, 34, 42, 43, 51, 55–60, 75, 85, 93, 94, 103, 114
2:13–17	10, 59, 60–61, 63, 75
2:13–14	56, 62
2:13—3:7	93
2:13	61, 62, 66, 74, 83
2:14–16	42
2:14–15	93, 94
2:14	93
2:15	43, 62, 70
2:16	42, 74
2:17	50, 56, 59, 62, 63, 64, 66, 67, 83, 86, 91
2:18–20	5, 21, 54, 64–68
2:18–19	10
2:18	5, 10, 59, 61, 64, 65, 66, 74, 83, 91
2:19–23	7
2:19	65–67, 83
2:20	7, 67, 69, 93, 94
2:21–25	15, 16, 30, 63, 68–72, 125
2:21–24	96
2:21–23	70
2:21	8, 14, 31, 40, 43, 47, 50, 51, 68, 74, 87, 93, 95, 102, 107
2:22–24	8, 37
2:22–23	70, 86
2:22	23, 68
2:22b–23	70
2:23	7, 21, 43, 68, 86, 91, 105, 114
2:24	19, 45, 68, 70
2:25	23, 68, 97
3:1–7	5, 74
3:1–6	59
3:1–2	10, 48, 55–59, 70, 74–76, 92, 93, 94, 114
3:1	33, 58, 61, 75, 76, 82, 83
3:2	33, 34, 58, 64, 67, 79, 83, 91
3:3–4	78–79
3:3	5, 79, 119
3:4	79, 80, 91
3:5–6	79–82
3:5	32, 34, 61, 91
3:6	10, 64, 79–81, 93
3:7	55, 74, 82–84, 107
3:8–12	84–88
3:8	43, 74, 84, 93
3:9–12	42, 63, 90, 92, 94
3:9–10	43, 94
3:9	7, 8, 51, 69, 70, 85–87, 112
3:10–12	91, 93
3:10	70
3:11	63, 92–94, 128
3:12	92
3:13–17	5, 90–93, 96
3:13–16	77
3:13	90, 93
3:14–17	10

3:14	7, 64, 67, 71, 91–93, 111	4:15–16	8
3:15–16	62, 75, 90, 92, 94	4:15	7, 42, 55, 56, 68, 71, 72, 74, 84, 85, 93, 112
3:15	8, 48, 51, 64, 91		
3:16–17	93, 94	4:16	8, 21, 55, 59, 69, 93, 112
3:16	8, 43, 55, 70, 79, 92, 93		
		4:17–19	58
3:17–22	58	4:17–18	20, 21
3:17–18	7	4:17	113, 123
3:17	7, 21, 42, 68, 90	4:19	7, 23, 70, 93, 94, 113, 123, 124
3:18–22	95–100, 114, 122		
3:18–19	97, 98	4:20	8
3:18	69, 70, 102	5:1–5	5, 72, 116–22
3:19–20	105	5:1	7, 21, 116, 119
3:19	100	5:4	21, 72, 116
3:20–21	80	5:5	61, 74, 82, 83, 91, 119
3:20	23, 98		
3:21	99	5:6–11	122–26
3:22	46, 61, 98, 123	5:6	91
4:1–6	101–6, 107	5:7	39, 72
4:1–2	71, 96	5:8–9	7
4:1	7	5:8	21, 29, 30, 98, 103, 107, 125
4:2	102, 103		
4:3–4	5, 21, 30	5:9	5, 7, 50, 114
4:3	6, 8, 10, 55, 56, 60, 71, 72, 74, 93, 102, 109	5:10	7, 20–22, 41, 50, 51, 58, 68, 69, 87, 116, 122, 124
4:4	6, 8, 10, 93, 111	5:11	22, 109, 122, 126
4:5–6	21	5:12–14	126–28
4:5	45	5:12	5, 7, 11, 14, 29, 40, 43
4:6	45		
4:7–11	74, 106–9, 119	5:13–14	33
4:7	29, 55, 103, 106–9, 123, 124	5:14	128
4:8–11	107	**2 Peter**	
4:8	39, 64	1:21	108
4:9	121	2:4	98
4:11	22, 108, 122	2:5	99
4:12–19	5, 8, 21, 110–14	2:9	7
4:12–17	10	3:6	99
4:12—5:11	54	3:9	99
4:12	7, 22	3:16	108
4:13–14	116	3:18	109
4:13	7, 21, 22, 122		
4:14–16	7	**1 John**	
4:14	8, 21, 22, 59, 70, 111, 112	2:1	96

2:2	96
2:29	96
3:5	69
3:7	96
3:8	124
3:9	19
3:16	107
4:1	98
5:1–4	19

Jude
6	98

Revelation
2:10	7, 124
3:10	7
3:12	46
5:12–13	22
11:1	46
12:9	124
12:12	124
14:8	127
16:19	127
17:5	127
18	128
18:2–21	127
19:7	21
20:2	124
20:7	98
20:10	124
21:4	101

APOCRYPHAL / DEUTEROCANONICAL BOOKS

Tobit
8:5	62
8:13	62

Judith
6:16	104
13:13	104
14:3	104
15:12	104

Wisdom of Solomon
5:18	42
13:1	6
14:18	6
14:22–27	104
17:2	34
18:15	42

Sirach/Ecclesiasticus
44:20	7, 21

1 Maccabees
2:52	7, 21

2 Maccabees
3:19	104
6:3–7	104
6:11	104
8:35	42
13:23	61

PSEUDEPIGRAPHA

Apocalypse of Baruch
10.1–3	127
11.1	127
67.7	127

1 Enoch
6–10	98
18:12—19:2	98

4 Ezra
3.1	127
3.28	127
3.31	127

Jubilees
7:21	98
22:16–18	31

Sibylline Oracles
5.143–68   127
5.434   127

Testament of Reuben
5.1–5   79

DEAD SEA SCROLLS

1QH—Hodayot
2.18–19   32

1 QpHab—Pesher Habakkuk
11.13   32

1QS—Serek Hayahad
5.1   32
5.10–13   32
5.15–20   32
7.24–25   32
8.11   32

CD—Cairo Genizah
6.14–15   32

PHILO

De cherubim
1.92   104

De decalogo
168   61

De sacrificiis Abelis et Caini
21   79

De virtutibus
39–40   79

JOSEPHUS

Antiquities
8.266   42

Against Apion
2.201   61

RABBINIC WRITINGS

Genesis Rabbah
47:1   80
52:5   80

APOSTOLIC FATHERS

Barnabas
4.2   104
19.4   79
19.7   65
20.1   42
20.2   43

1 Clement
13.1   42
13.4   79
16.10   42
22.3   42
30.1   43
30.3   43
35.5   42, 43
35.8   104
38:1   61
44.3–6   119
47.6   119
50.6   42
54.2b   119

2 Clement
6.1   66
17.5   104

Didache

4.10	65
5.1	42
15.1	118

Diognetus

1	50
1:3	86
5.15	86
9:2	96

Shepherd of Hermas, Mandate(s)

2.1.2–3	43
8.1.3	43

Shepherd of Hermas, Similitude(s)

9.15.3	43
23.2–3	43

Ignatius, *To the Ephesians*

3.2	104
4.1	104
7.1	42
10.1–3	59

Ignatius, *To Polycarp*

4.3	65
8.1	42

Martyrdom of Polycarp

2.2	43
4.3	43
6.1	104
13.2	42

Polycarp, *To the Philippians*

5.2	118

GRECO-ROMAN WRITINGS

Aesop
Fabulae

3	94

Apuleius
Metamorphoses

3.12	113

Aristotle
Ethica eudemia

1233b20–26	43

Ethica nicomachea

4.5	79

Oeconomica

1.5–6	65
3.1	78

Politica

1.5.3–11	64

Rhetorica

1386b18–19	43

Topica

90	86

Cicero
De officiis

2.19.6	111

Epistulae ad Atticum

11:5	2

Epistulae ad familiares

16.10.2	2

Horace
Satirae

1.1.77	111

Juvenal

Satirae
14.104–5   32

Ovid

Ars amatoria
3.136–38   78

Phintys

Concerning the Temperance of a Woman
153.15–28   78

Plato

Gorgias
491D   107

Pliny the Elder

Naturalis historia
33.6.26–27   65
33.19.59   22

Pliny the Younger

Epistulae
10.96   11
10.96.2   8
10.97.1   8

Seneca

De Providentia
5.10   22

Epistulae morales
47   64

Strabo

Geographica
16.1.5   128

Tacitus

Annales
15.44   60
15.44.2–5   111

Historiae
5.5   32

Varro

On Agriculture
1.17   64

Xenophon

Memorabilia
2.1.16   65

EARLY CHRISTIAN WRITINGS

Clement of Alexandria

Stromateis
6.5.41   50

Eusebius

Historia ecclesiastica
5.1.7   60

Justin

Dialogue with Trypho
17   96
110.4   11

Prima Apologia
14:3   52

Tertullian

Ad nationes
1.7.8   60
1.8   50

Apologeticus
37.8   60

Apology
3   76